SLIM & SCRUMPTIOUS

Also by Joy Bauer

Joy Bauer's Food Cures
Joy's LIFE Diet
Your Inner Skinny

SLIM & SCRUMPTIOUS

More Than 75 Delicious, **Healthy Meals** Your Family Will Love

JOY BAUER

Photographs by Joseph DeLeo

WILLIAM MORROW
An Imprint of HarperCollins Publishers

This book is intended to be informational and should not be considered a substitute for advice from a medical professional, whom the reader should consult before beginning any diet or exercise regimen, and before taking any dietary
supplements or other medication. The author and publisher expressly disclaim responsibility for any adverse effects
arising from the use or application of the information contained in this book.

HarperCollins books may be purchased for educational, business, or sales promotional use. For information please write:
Special Markets Department, HarperCollins Publishers, 10 East 53rd Street, New York, NY 10022.

FIRST EDITION

Designed by Lorie Pagnozzi

Library of Congress Cataloging-in-Publication Data has been applied for.

ISBN 978-0-06-183477-6

10 11 12 13 14 WBC/RRD 10 9 8 7 6 5 4 3

To my mom, Ellen Schloss, for her grace, selflessness, and love—and for teaching me the value of a home-cooked family meal.

CONTENTS

HEARTY STEWS, CHILIS & BURGERS 63

- White Chili Fiesta
- Brazilian Seafood Stew
- Italian Chicken and Sausage Stew
- Ratatouille Lentil Stew
- Buffalo Chicken Chili with Whipped Blue Cheese
- Tandoori Chicken Burgers with Carrot Raita
- Garden Lentil Burgers

PASTA ENTRÉES 81

- AJ's Mac-n-Cheezy
- Turkey Tetrazzini
- Chicken Fettuccine Alfredo with Sun-Dried Tomatoes
- Summery Pesto Pasta
- Pasta with Turkey Bolognese
- Halibut and Rotini with Spring Pea Puree
- Spaghetti with Shrimp and Fennel

POULTRY ENTRÉES 101

- Chicken Lettuce Wraps
- Mediterranean Meatloaf
- Chipotle Chicken
- Upside-Down Pan Pizza with the Works
- Sesame Chicken Tenders
- Chicken Cacciatore
- Joy's Turkey Meatballs with Easy Marinara Sauce
- Braised Turkey Sausage and Cabbage
- Chicken Cordon Bleu
- Turkey Thyme Meatballs with Lemony Cream Sauce
- Lemon-Sage Chicken Breasts
- Crispy Parmesan Chicken

BEEF & PORK ENTRÉES 135

FISH & SEAFOOD ENTRÉES 151

VEGGIE SIDES 171

SNACKS & SWEETS 189

SLIM & SCRUMPTIOUS

INTRODUCTION

If only we each had our very own mealtime fairy godmother, someone with the culinary wisdom and motherly warmth of a cross between Julia Child and Mary Poppins. At 5 o'clock sharp each night, the heavens would open up and she'd magically swoop into the house, groceries in tow, and whip up the most smashingly delicious, 100% nutritious dinner. And of course, she would leave the kitchen sparkling clean. Sigh . . .

Like you, I juggle way too many balls as I go from one day to the next. I have three active kids, a demanding full-time job, a wonderful husband, and scores of responsibilities that require my attention. There are plenty of days when I'm in over my head and feel like I'll never find time to make dinner, and yet I nearly always do. And, day in and day out, I'm glad I

made the effort. Trust me—you will be, too.

Cooking healthful everyday meals for your family may herald a lifestyle change for you and the rest of your brood. Whether you're already comfortable in the kitchen but looking for more nutritious recipes to replace some of your current family favorites, or you're a culinary novice who wants to learn how to make delicious, wholesome, and foolproof meals, you've come to the right place.

Full disclosure: I'm a nutritionist and a mom, not a culinary expert (and far from the next Iron Chef!). But that's good news for you, and here's why: I've gone out of my way to ensure that the recipes in this book produce fabulous, flavorful results without requiring complicated prep or advanced technique. And while it's true that cooking can be a time investment, particularly at first, the payoff is significant. Your food costs will go down, everyone will feel and look better, and mealtimes will become joyful parts of the day filled with family togetherness. And in my opinion, few things rank higher than hearing my kids compliment or special-request one of my latest creations ("Please can we have Sesame Chicken Tenders for dinner tonight?"). It's true—cooking healthful food can be easy and gratifying.

Good News! Cooking at Home Is Better for You

You can't control what your kids select on the school's hot lunch line, the junk food they eat at their friend's house, or the sugar-laden birthday cupcakes they devour in the classroom—and you certainly can't stop your husband from ordering his favorite chicken parm sub and chips at the local sandwich shop—but fortunately you *can* control what your family eats in your own home. Here, within your own four walls, you get to call all the shots when it comes to minimizing the not-so-healthy ingredients and maximizing the healthy.

ADDED FATS, like the butter, oil, and margarine used to sauté, roast, and fry food, are one of the main offenders behind high-cal meals. As a college student I held my fair share

of waitressing jobs, so I've witnessed firsthand the frightening amount of fat that goes into restaurant meals (and much of it is the artery-clogging saturated type). First there's the butter they sauté the veggies in, then there's the oil they baste the meat with, then the cream and extra butter that finds its way into sauces and side dishes . . . sometimes there's even a generous drizzle of olive oil to finish off the plate. And most of the time all that extra fat is overkill. For the recipes in this book, I go out of my way to minimize *all* fats, even the heart-healthy oils like olive and canola. While it's true that unsaturated plant oils have beneficial health effects, they're still extremely calorie-dense, which means that liberal usage can easily add hundreds of calories to your meals over the course of a week. To make a little bit of fat go a long way, I use oil spray for sautéing, roasting, and greasing pans. When you adopt this strategy instead of pouring oil directly from the bottle, you'll effortlessly slash calories from your diet on a daily basis.

SALT levels in restaurant meals and convenience foods are over the top. In fact, when you are dining out, there's a good chance the entrée alone contains enough salt to exceed your sodium allotment for the entire day, which is no more than 2,300 milligrams for healthy adults. Since a high-salt diet is linked to high blood pressure, an increased risk of some cancers, water retention, and bloating, it's definitely in your best interest to prepare lower-sodium meals at home. Nearly all of my recipes contain less than 800 milligrams of sodium per serving, so they're in perfect alignment with government standards for healthy entrées. Unlike carbohydrates, fiber, protein, and fat, which are all measured in grams, you'll notice that sodium is measured in the much smaller unit of milligrams—that's why sodium numbers seem so much higher than other values on nutrition labels.

To keep sodium levels in check, I use low-sodium versions of the saltiest offenders like broth, canned tomatoes and beans, and soy sauce in my recipes. When I add salt to a dish, I season sparingly and always use kosher salt, which has a coarser grain than fine table salt and therefore yields less sodium per teaspoon. Sea salt works equally well, but be sure to purchase a coarse-grained variety. Though I realize *some* salt is usually necessary to make food that much more delicious, my intent is to help you retrain your palate so that it is excited by other seasonings and not controlled by the tyranny of salt.

LEAN CUTS OF MEAT are another staple ingredient in healthy cooking. When you dine out or choose prepared foods, you're at the mercy of the chef's or food manufacturer's protein selections, and these guys have a big economic incentive to use cheaper, fattier cuts of meat. Think about it: how many diners make their burgers with 95% lean ground sirloin? When was the last time your fast-food breakfast sandwich came with lean turkey sausage instead of a cheap, high-fat pork patty? If you do go out of your way to order lean proteins, like lean steak, seafood, or fish, at a restaurant, expect to pay much more than it would cost for you to prepare these entrées in your own kitchen. When you prepare meals at home, you can make selections that are both budget- and waistline-friendly, like skinless poultry, ground turkey and chicken, affordable fish and seafood, and lean cuts of pork and beef. Yup, you heard right, *beef!* If you were worried that red meat wouldn't make an appearance in a nutritionist-approved cookbook, fear no longer. I respect the fact that many of my readers love beef—my husband, Ian, is among you!—so I have not neglected the category at all. In fact, the Beef and Bell Pepper Stir-Fry on page 137 and the Beef Tenderloin with Fig Reduction on page 143 are among Ian's all-time favorite recipes. I hope you'll give them a try.

LIGHT CONDIMENTS are an effective way to slash calories and fat in everyday cooking. Fortunately, most of our favorite fat-laden brands are also available in slimmed-down versions. For example, I regularly use reduced-fat mayo, sour cream, and cream cheese in my recipes. Because these dishes are already packed with delicious, fresh flavors, you won't for a second miss the extra fat. Choosing light versions of the condiments you use on a regular basis is one of the simplest ways to give your cooking a healthy facelift.

FRESH, WHOLESOME FOODS, without preservatives and other unnecessary additives and artificial colors, are flat-out good for you. Choosing foods that are not overly processed, that are in season, and that are close to their original form means you are in charge of what does and does not go into the meals your family eats. The more you cook with whole ingredients like fruits, vegetables, and grains, the more you'll appreciate the clean, fresh flavors of *real food*.

PORTION CONTROL has become downright out of control. At restaurants, we've grown to expect gargantuan plates filled with ridiculous amounts of food, and more often than not, we wipe our plates clean regardless of whether we're truly all that hungry. With this in mind, I've suggested a healthful *yet satisfying* portion size for every recipe in this book. What's more, when you follow my portion

guidelines, you'll often have leftovers to serve the next day, which is a smart way to trim your food budget as well as your waistline.

Cooking at Home Is Good for the Family

At the end of a long day of running here, there, and everywhere, there's nothing I look forward to more than sitting down to a relaxing, gab-filled dinner with my family. As much as I appreciate the health benefits of cooking in, it's the time I get to spend chatting and connecting with my husband and kids that really motivates me to make mealtime a priority. When dinnertime strikes, all of our otherwise divergent paths intersect and for thirty (perhaps uninterrupted) minutes, we get to put life on pause. Clearly, the kitchen table is the heartbeat of our home.

In addition to sharing meals with my kids, I love to cook alongside them whenever I get the chance. My kids are getting older—Jesse, Cole, and Ayden Jane are fifteen, twelve, and nine, respectively—so they are pretty competent in the kitchen at this point. It took some time to build up their skills, but years of working together have paid off and now I don't hesitate to ask my youngest to measure out ingredients or my older ones to cut vegetables or stir a simmering pot, or even to flip pancakes.

I think of the time we spend in the kitchen as "found time" when we can chat freely about school, friends, movies, and sports. Sometimes I can even take advantage of the moment to squeeze out a juicy bit of teenage gossip that I would never be privy to otherwise!

While this all sounds great in theory, I fully understand that kids have sports, homework, dance classes, and other after-school commitments, so cooking together on weekday evenings isn't always an option. If that's the case, try to set aside some time over the weekend to prepare breakfast, brunch, or dinner together as a family.

Depending on our schedule, I try to let each of my kids plan the dinner menu for one night of the week. This routine gets them excited about mealtime and allows them to take ownership of that night's dish (plus, it's one less decision for me to make!). When it comes to preparing the food, we really have fun. We clear the counters of the day's clutter, throw on some music (I have a cute jukebox right next to the sink for just this purpose), and break out the pots and pans. I cherish the opportunity for some one-on-one time with my kids, and Jesse, Cole, and Ayden gain a sense of accomplishment each and every time they deliver their final product to the table. It's a win-win situation.

This strategy also encourages little ones to eat foods they might not ordinarily try. When you make something a little outside your kids' comfort zone, be sure to get them involved in the prep. If they help prepare it, I promise, they will be much more willing to taste it. For instance, my daughter Ayden was a bit skeptical of the Chicken Lettuce Wraps on page 103 because there were "too many things" in them. I passed her my food chopper and let her mince the ingredients all by herself (with my close supervision, of course). She devoured the wraps at dinner that night and asked for them again a week later. I was thrilled.

Of course, it won't always be this easy—you may have to get creative in order to convince your picky eaters to try new foods or recipes. My best advice is to speak their language. In other words, figure out what interests your kids most and then work it to your advantage. Ayden loves sports, so I'm forever explaining how protein fuels her muscles, making her stronger and faster on the soccer field. Jesse, on the other hand, is a fashionista, so when I talk about nutrient-dense vegetables that provide the right ingredients for radiant skin and thick, shiny hair, her ears perk up and she's ready to give them a try. Lesson learned: When it comes to getting your brood to try new healthy foods, where there's a will, there's a way.

The power of food is endless. As a health professional, I am particularly interested in how eating together and eating right affects overall family dynamics. Spending quality time gathered around the table, enjoying healthy food and conversation, can tighten your family bond, encourage ongoing communication, improve physical health, and keep everyone's weight in check. For me, cooking is even therapeutic . . . for real! If you're not already reaping these incredible benefits, do your family a favor and get started today.

Eating at Home Saves Money

I hear it all the time: cooking healthy costs a lot of money. Unfortunately, there is some truth to this common complaint; fresh produce and lean meats can be costly relative to less nutritious foods. That said, if you follow three simple strategies, it is definitely possible to eat well *affordably*.

Strategy #1. Make most of your meals at home.

When you dine at restaurants, you pay a significant upcharge for service and ambiance, not to mention all the extras like beverages, appetizers, and desserts that you inevitably find yourself ordering once tempted by the server or the menu. Plus, eating out rarely yields leftovers. Most people are accustomed to finishing off their entire entrée, and even if they are restrained enough to leave food on their plate, they may decide it's more convenient to let extras go to waste than to lug around a doggie bag for the rest of the night. When you cook at home and serve appropriate portions, you can stretch your meals (and your food dollars) by having leftovers for lunch or dinner the following day.

These days, you can buy convenience and packaged food just about anywhere (even the hardware store). It's all too easy to swipe a credit card for snacks, drinks, and other impulse food purchases as you move through the day, so you'll have to work hard to make buying food from locations other than the grocery store the exception rather than the norm. But without a doubt, the greater the proportion of your food that comes from your own kitchen—rather than the drugstore, gas station, office cafeteria, street vendor, drive-thru, or local bakery—the lower your food costs will be.

Strategy #2. Become a savvy shopper.

If you're cooking at home more often, you'll certainly be spending more at the supermarket, but there are plenty of smart ways to cut back on your grocery bill. First, stock up when items you use regularly go on sale, and store them in your pantry or freezer. When your store offers a great deal on chicken breasts or ground turkey, buy two or three packages instead of just one and stash them in your freezer. If staples like broth, canned beans and vegetables, whole grain pasta, frozen vegetables, cereal, or oft-used condiments are on special, buy extras and stockpile them for later. Most of us are so busy that we've trained ourselves to live day-to-day and not plan for grocery needs down the road, but with a little foresight you can save a bundle on commonly used ingredients.

Buying in bulk at club stores can also save you money, but make sure you only purchase items you know you're going to use. I've seen so many people load up on multi-packs of ingredients that have a great unit price but end up going to waste because they never find ways to use them. Wherever you shop, buy generic whenever possible. There's usually no difference in quality compared to more expensive branded items, whose prices are inflated partly because national manufacturers are passing on their marketing expenses to you and other customers. If lowering food costs is a priority, you'll also want to bypass healthy food that has been processed for convenience. For example, instead of buying pre-cut stir-fry vegetables in the produce department, buy the vegetables whole and chop them yourself. Purchase foods like yogurt and oatmeal in large containers, which are significantly cheaper than individual, pre-portioned containers or packets. Rather than pay a hefty premium for the grocery store or manufacturer to perform extra labor, do the work yourself and pocket the difference in cost. There's always going to be a trade-off between cost and convenience, but if saving money is important to you, it's worth the effort to do more of the prep yourself.

Strategy #3. Grow your own food.

If you have the space and the inclination, or have been inspired by the recent push for eating local, plant your own garden. Over time, this is a fabulous way to cut down on the cost of fresh produce and to guarantee that much of the food you eat is optimally nutritious. If you don't have the time or the area to commit to a full garden plot, consider planting a few fresh herbs in pots that can sit on the windowsill or deck. It's far less costly to buy a small potted plant once a year or so than to buy cut fresh herbs from the market on a weekly basis. Plus, there's the added convenience of being able to spontaneously snip a few leaves to add to a recipe whenever you like.

The Skinny on Some Must-Have Ingredients

Here you'll find information on the foods I get questioned about the most. This isn't a comprehensive grocery list, but rather a quick guide to some key ingredients that will slenderize your kitchen. I also elaborate on ingredients in many of my recipe notes, so if you don't find certain information here, chances are you will when you cook a specific dish.

LOW-FAT DAIRY: For most types of dairy—milk, yogurt, sour cream, and cream cheese—I encourage people to purchase low-fat *or* nonfat, whichever variety suits their family's preferences. If the nonfat versions simply don't cut it in your house, recognize that reduced-fat cream cheese, light sour cream, and 1% low-fat milk are still nutritious options that fit into an overall healthy diet.

When it comes to cheese, I shy away from using fat-free varieties in my recipes. Nonfat cheese usually has an unappealing rubbery texture and just doesn't melt well. Instead, I recommend using reduced-fat cheeses made with 2% milk (or "part skim" for mozzarella and ricotta). The payoff for that extra bit of fat is huge; it gives cheeses like cheddar and Swiss a creamier mouthfeel and helps them to melt beautifully. So, while I always encourage people to drink milk that's skim or 1%, I find it's actually preferable to choose cheeses made from 2% milk. Every good rule has an exception, and mine is Parmesan cheese. I buy the authentic, full-fat version. It has such a strong, sharp taste that a little goes a long way, and I think it's worth the extra calories.

• *Fat-free evaporated milk* is made by removing about 50% of the water from skim milk. What's left behind is a creamier and thicker milk product, still without a drop of fat. I love the extra richness and body evaporated milk gives to soups and sauces, so you'll find it used in a number of my recipes. Unlike perishable dairy products, it comes in shelf-stable cans, so take advantage and stock up when it's on sale. If you don't use up the entire can for a recipe, transfer the remainder to a storage container and keep it in the fridge; it's a great alternative to regular milk in coffee. Word to the wise: Don't confuse it with sweetened condensed milk (loaded with sugar and calories), which is usually located right next to the evaporated milk on the grocery shelf and comes in remarkably similar looking cans. My poor husband, Ian, has picked up the wrong can by mistake on more than one occasion!

• *Buttermilk* is a fabulous ingredient for low-fat cooking and baking. Though it has a thick, creamy texture, buttermilk is actually very low in fat . . . and no, it isn't made from butter! Commercial buttermilk is produced by adding live cultures to skim or low-fat milk. It's the culturing process, not a high fat content, that makes buttermilk so rich and creamy. Buttermilk has a characteristically tangy flavor and is more acidic than plain milk, so you won't want to substitute one for the other in recipes.

CANNED GOODS: Let me start by debunking a popular nutrition myth: *canned vegetables are not inherently less nutritious than fresh* (although you do have to be careful about sodium levels). I love the convenience of canned goods and always keep a supply of canned beans, tomatoes, and broth, to name a few of my must-haves, in my pantry.

• *Canned beans* are a busy cook's best friend. You will certainly cut your cost if you buy dried beans and soak and cook them yourself, but the canned ones save a lot of time and are still an affordable option. Buy low-sodium beans if they're available, but don't fret if they're not. Thoroughly rinsing canned beans under running water will wash away a good amount of the salt. I find myself cooking with chickpeas and black beans most often, but all varieties are equally nutritious.

• *Canned tomatoes* are another convenience I couldn't live without. During the summer,

when farmers' markets, roadside stands, and backyard gardens are bursting with sun-kissed tomatoes, I use fresh whenever possible, but the rest of the year I rely on canned. I tested all the recipes in this book with "no salt added" tomatoes. If you can't find them at your store, go ahead and use salt-added tomatoes but reduce or entirely omit the salt in the recipe. Let your taste buds be your guide.

• *Canned broth* is a true kitchen must-have—you'll notice I use it over and over again throughout the book. Unfortunately, regular broth (all types—beef, chicken, and vegetable) is loaded with salt. One cup can have nearly 1,000 milligrams of sodium (almost half your allowance for the entire day!). For this reason, I always call for unsalted or low-sodium broth. While I've never had the patience to make stock from scratch, if you do, huge kudos. You get to call the shots when it comes to added salt.

Because canned broth literally lasts for years in the pantry, I load up my cart when I catch a good sale. You'll save yourself a bundle, and because it's such an all-purpose ingredient, it's good to always have an ample supply on hand. By the way, when I say "canned broth" I also mean the kind packaged in aseptic boxes. The boxes are great because once opened, you can reseal and pop them in the fridge for up to a week, which is super-convenient when you just need a few tablespoons here and there.

WHOLE GRAINS: By choosing whole grains over refined, you dramatically improve the nutritional profile of your meals. Whole grains contain all three parts of the grain's kernel: the fiber- and antioxidant-rich outer bran, the vitamin- and mineral-packed germ, and the starchy endosperm. Refined grains, on the other hand, contain only the endosperm of the seed, meaning that the most nutritious components of the grain have been removed during processing. Despite the added health benefits you get when you switch from refined to whole grains, there's almost no added expense: whole wheat bread, whole grain pasta, and brown rice cost pennies more (if that) than their refined counterparts.

There are lots of underused whole grains worth learning about, such as bulgur, wheat berries, quinoa, farro, and whole wheat couscous (which is actually a pasta), but here I chose to concentrate on those that are most familiar and most common to the recipes in this cookbook.

• *Whole wheat flour* comes in a few varieties: standard whole wheat flour, whole wheat pastry flour, and whole wheat bread flour. You'll find that most of my recipes call for standard whole wheat flour, which is the most readily available of the three. However, you may want to become familiar with whole wheat pastry flour too, since I've noticed it's showing up in recipes with greater frequency. Whole wheat pastry flour is milled from soft wheat, which produces a silkier, finer flour that's better for making pastries and cakes than the all-purpose type. If you can't find whole wheat pastry flour on the baking aisle, it may be hiding out in the natural foods section of your supermarket. One last note: Because whole wheat flours go rancid faster than refined versions, you'll want to store them in the fridge or freezer to maximize shelf life.

• *Oats* come in two basic forms: rolled oats (available in old-fashioned, quick-cooking, and instant varieties) and steel-cut oats, both of which are whole grain products. Steel-cut oats are produced by cutting whole oat groats into pieces, rather than steaming them and rolling them flat. For this reason, steel-cut oats take longer to cook than rolled oats and yield a thicker, heartier oatmeal. While both rolled and steel-cut oats are wonderful served as hot cereal, you'll want to stick with rolled oats when making quick-cooking baked goods like cookies, muffins, and pancakes.

• *Brown rice* get its color, nutty taste, and slight crunch from the grain's bran and germ, the two nutrient-rich parts of the kernel that get stripped away and discarded in order to create white rice. Regular brown rice takes longer to cook than white, but quick-cooking versions are now available for days when you're crunched for time. To maximize value, buy brown rice in the large bags instead of boxes; they'll keep for a good 6 months in your pantry.

• *Whole wheat pastas* are making their presence known on supermarket shelves everywhere. I applaud this, although I know not everyone shares my enthusiasm—many of my friends and clients complain that whole wheat pastas taste gummy or chewy. That being said, they are so much better for your overall health that it really is worth it to make the switch. With just a little time and a few good recipes, your taste buds will acclimate and you'll wholeheartedly embrace these healthful pantry staples.

To identify 100% whole wheat pastas, look for brands that include only flours preceded by the word "whole." If you're looking for a middle ground, try a whole wheat blend, which contains a mix of whole and refined wheat flour; just be sure that either the first or second flour is preceded by the word "whole." Another healthy alternative is pastas made from a combination of grains, beans, lentils, and even ground flaxseed (just check the ingredients list for these superstar additions). These interesting pasta blends have an appearance and flavor similar to that of traditional pasta, and while they're not entirely whole grain,

they have considerably more protein and fiber than the pure refined type, so I consider them a substantial nutritional improvement. Thanks to growing consumer demand for whole grain options, most supermarkets now stock all three pasta categories in a variety of popular shapes, from linguine to penne to fusilli.

LEAN PROTEINS: Although there are a few delicious vegetarian recipes in this cookbook, the majority of the main entrées feature lean animal proteins: eggs, skinless and ground poultry, lean cuts of red meat, and fish and shellfish. From a nutritional standpoint, the meat and fish counters can be the most confusing section of the grocery store if you don't know exactly what to look for. Here's the essential information you'll need to make healthy protein selections going forward.

• *Eggs* have gotten a bad rap over the years, but they're actually a healthful, protein-rich addition to a balanced diet. I recognize that egg yolks have a meaningful amount of saturated fat and cholesterol, so I typically use a combination of just a few yolks and mostly whites in egg dishes. Here's a general rule of thumb for making egg substitutions in recipes: 1 whole egg=2 egg whites or ¼ cup of egg substitute.

• *Ground meat* should be at least 90% lean. This rule holds true for ground turkey, ground chicken, and ground beef. Unfortunately, as the percent lean goes up, so does the price tag. With that in mind, you'll usually get your best buy on healthy ground meats that fall between 90% and 95% lean. If extra-lean ground meat (96% to 99%) goes on sale, by all means stock up and store it in your freezer, but please don't feel bad if your budget can't swing the extra-lean variety on a regular basis. In my opinion, the small difference in fat content is not worth the premium.

• *Skinless poultry* plays the leading role in many of my recipes. While most of us think of white poultry meat as being far more healthful than dark, this simply is not the case once the skin is removed. In fact, for a standard serving, the difference in saturated fat content is minimal. Though breast meat is by far my own personal favorite (as well as my kids'), I also appreciate the juiciness and meaty flavor of chicken thighs. The majority of my chicken dishes call for breasts, but if you're a dark-meat lover, feel free to substitute skinless thighs.

• *Lean beef and pork* offer a variety of vitamins and minerals essential for good health, most notably high-quality iron. When it comes to beef, cuts with the terms "loin" or "round" in the name, such as sir*loin* and top and bottom *round,* are your leanest options. For pork, I say go for the tenderloin. Not only is it the leanest and tenderest cut, it's also fast-cooking and a great canvas for marinades and seasonings.

• *Fish and shellfish* are some of the best choices for healthful lean proteins, and I'm always encouraging people to make fish a more frequent feature in their dinner rotation. But you do have to be careful about what you buy. The trouble is, we are overfishing many of our waters and contaminating others, making some fish environmentally unsound or unsafe to eat. I recommend visiting the following websites to find out which seafood is most eco-friendly and lowest in toxins:

• The Environmental Defense Fund
 edf.org/page.cfm?tagID=1521
• National Resources Defense Council
 nrdc.org/health/effects/mercury/guide.asp
• Monterey Bay Seafood Watch
 montereybayaquarium.org/cr/cr_
 seafoodwatch/download.aspx

FLAVOR ENHANCERS: I look for condiments and other flavor enhancers that add volumes of flavor for an insignificant amount of calories, thus giving you the biggest bang for your buck. Here are a bunch of my favorites.

• *Hot sauces* are virtually calorie-free and heat up a dish like no other ingredient. My husband is a serious hot sauce aficionado and has accumulated quite a collection of regional and specialty bottles over the years, some of them too flaming hot for even *my* spice-loving taste buds! Lately, Ian and I have become big fans of sriracha, a Thai hot sauce you'll find in a handful of the recipes in this book. I often add a generous splash of hot sauce directly to my soups, stews, and casseroles while they're cooking. But if not everyone in your family appreciates fiery foods, leave it out of the dish and put in on the table instead—this way, people can adjust the heat to their own liking.

• *Soy sauce* adds a unique savory dimension that really deepens and intensifies a dish's flavor. I use it in all types of food, not just Asian cuisine. Of course, soy sauce's major drawback is its high sodium content. I suggest low-sodium versions, which have about half the sodium of regular soy sauce, but even these are high in salt and should be used judiciously.

• *Vinegars* have an unmatched ability to perk up dishes with their powerful hit of acidity. My favorite is sweet, rich balsamic, which I often use to dress salads or to finish dishes with a little zing. In addition, I suggest you have a good red wine vinegar, white wine vinegar, rice vinegar, and some apple cider vinegar on hand. A little goes a long way and the bottles keep forever in the pantry. Heads up: If you use your vinegars to make your own vinaigrette dressings, I suggest reducing the classic 3:1 ratio of oil to vinegar so that there are nearly

equal amounts of both. This trick will save you major calories and fat.

• *Herbs and spices* are invaluable when you're creating waistline-friendly, low-fat, low-sodium dishes. So-called health food can be bland and nondescript (okay, yes, even cardboard-like), but it certainly doesn't have to be. Fresh and dried herbs and spices add amazing flavor and more than make up for what's *not* going into your food (gobs of butter, loads of salt, and heaps of sugar). I love my old standbys—thyme, oregano, basil, chili powder, cumin, red pepper flakes, and cinnamon, to name a few—but lately I've had a lot of fun experimenting with others like cardamom, smoked paprika, chipotle and ancho chile powders, and turmeric, which you'll find scattered throughout these recipes. There are also some great spice blends out there, which are incredibly convenient because they allow you to add loads of flavor from just one jar. I say, when it comes to herbs and spices, let your creativity go wild!

Must-Have Cooking Tools

There's nothing like having the right tool for the job. When it comes to cooking equipment, you certainly don't have to outfit your kitchen with every gadget and gizmo out there (I've yet to see the utility of jalapeño corers or spinning spaghetti forks, for example), but you *should* stock up on good, sturdy tools that will make kitchen prep decidedly easier. By investing in the right gear, you'll spend less time chopping and cleaning and more time gathered around the dinner table enjoying your meal.

Many of these items are one-time purchases, so while I don't think you have to spend a fortune on them, you should aim for quality. Look for sales and coupons, and definitely take the time to read customer product reviews at popular online shopping websites before making your selections. Other users' experiences can be incredibly informative, and a little research will save you money and time.

Many of these tools make thoughtful presents—so don't be shy, go ahead and mention to your family or (super-close) friends what you'd like as a gift! My son, Cole, once gave me an inexpensive food chopper for Mother's Day, and I still maintain it's one of the best gifts I have ever received. Johannah, my company's director of research, gave me a citrus zester when we first began the recipe testing phase for this book. I absolutely love both tools and find they have made culinary jobs far, far easier than they were before.

Here is the kitchen equipment that I think you'll find most useful when preparing the recipes in this book. These tools will streamline your prep time *and* help make you a healthier cook.

- **Blenders:** Of course blenders are the tool of choice for homemade smoothies and frozen drinks, but they're also great for making sauces and pureed soups and for crushing ice. I suggest you buy a good one because the inexpensive models just don't have enough power behind them to get the job done.

- **Cutting boards:** When I first started to experiment in the kitchen as a young teen, my mother was always scolding me for cutting food directly on her countertops. Now that I have my own countertops (and realize what an expensive investment they are), I'm proud to say I've become a much more conscientious slicer.

  I'm a big fan of flexible cutting boards, which come in a lot of fun colors and are easy to store because they slither right into drawers or cupboards and take up very little space. I like to color-code my cutting boards: I use one for raw meat only, one for vegetables and strong-tasting ingredients such as garlic and onions, and another for fruit.

- **Food processors:** Food processors are considered standard kitchen equipment these days, and if you already own one, you know how useful they are for making sauces and dips and quickly shredding, chopping, or mincing large quantities of just about anything. While you can definitely buy a bigger model, for most of my needs I find a 4- to 7-cup processor works just fine and is small enough to store pretty much anywhere (I leave mine right on the kitchen counter).

- **Hand-operated food choppers:** This tool is *invaluable*, especially if you're new to the cooking scene and haven't mastered your knife skills yet. It's so easy to operate; just by pumping the blade with your hand a few times you can quickly dice onions, garlic, celery, tomatoes, hard-boiled eggs . . . you name it. It makes chopping veggies easier than ever because you have complete control over the size of the chop and can produce small pieces without being an expert with a knife. The blade is well shielded, so it's safe for young kids to use. Plus, it's easy to clean and will even give your biceps and triceps a mini workout (you'll have Michelle Obama arms in no time!).

- **Immersion blenders:** Immersion blenders (also called "stick" or "handheld" blenders) are great if you like to make pureed soups, like the Creamy Curried Cauliflower and Cream of Broccoli soups in this book. Immersion blenders are designed to puree food right in the pot, which allows you to skip

the step of transferring hot liquids to a standard blender in batches, thus saving you time and extra dirty dishes. This is another tool kids like to play with, so it's one more good way to engage them in the kitchen.

- **Knives:** If you're an everyday home cook like me, you definitely don't need to invest in a fancy twenty-piece knife collection—half of them will never even leave the block. I suggest a handful of paring knives, a good chef's knife, and a serrated knife, but most of all I recommend *sharp* knives! A sharp knife is far safer than a dull one, which requires extra force to cut with and can easily slip and cause injury. Invest in a good knife sharpener, too, so that you can keep the blades keen and effective. I've had great success with an inexpensive, handheld manual sharpener.

- **Measuring utensils:** In my opinion, you can never have too many measuring spoons, scoops, and cups, particularly since it's so important to measure ingredients accurately when you are watching calories and fat. And since it's no fun to hunt through a crowded drawer for a tiny lone teaspoon (I speak from experience here), it's worth stocking your kitchen with multiple sets. For measuring dry ingredients like flour and sugar I particularly like measuring scoops, which minimize spills and messes. I'm notorious for throwing the kitchen into disarray when I cook, so I'll take all the help I can get.

- **Microplane zesters:** Citrus peel, or zest, is a fantastic, calorie-free way to give dishes a shot of bright flavor. However, without the right tool for the job, many people skip this ingredient in recipes to save time. Believe me, you won't hesitate to embrace this important flavor enhancer once you've invested in a handheld Microplane zester. This clever little gadget zests oranges, lemons, and limes in seconds flat and is much easier to clean than a full-sized box grater. I even use mine to grate ginger (and sometimes garlic) right into the pan.

- **Oil misters:** My absolute favorite thing about oil misters is the oodles of calories they save. A few years ago, I purchased a refillable oil mister to permanently replace the costly disposable canisters of cooking spray I was constantly buying. As I mentioned before, using spray oil instead of pouring bottled oil directly into pots and pans will trim down the calories in your recipes significantly (olive and canola oils are my oils of choice).

Cost-effective, environmentally friendly, and calorie-smart. What's not to love?

- **Pots and pans:** While you don't need an expensive set of matching cookware, you will need a variety of pots and pans to meet all of your cooking needs. For my recipes, I suggest a 10- to 12-quart stockpot, or an even bigger one if you entertain a lot and make large quantities of stews and chilis. I use 2- to 3-quart saucepans for sauces and reheating; a 12- to 14-inch sloping-sided skillet (large enough to hold four good-sized chicken breasts in a single layer) for pan-searing, and a similarly sized straight-sided sauté pan for sautéing large quantities of food. Be sure to have several good, heavy baking sheets that won't warp, and a roomy roasting pan. I also have several overproof casserole dishes and find the most useful size is 9×13 inches.

In the Kitchen with the Kids

Even when my kids were still in high chairs, I found ways to include them while I was busy in the kitchen. I remember handing them pieces of food, mixing spoons, and plastic bowls so they could mimic me as I cooked. To really make it fun, I bought each of them a cute little apron and chef toque to wear while they helped out. I dragged chairs over from the kitchen table for the kids to stand on, so even with their short little legs they could reach over the counters and help me toss salads or stir ingredients. When the kids got a little older, I let them drop cookie batter onto baking sheets and shape burgers and meatballs. The finished product was usually far from perfect (understatement!), but I constantly reminded myself it was the experience that mattered most.

When you include kids in the kitchen, they develop valuable skills that will last them into adulthood, so I suggest you make every effort to get them involved regardless of their age or ability. To get you (and them) started, I've outlined a handful of age-appropriate cooking tasks you can delegate to your little chefs-in-training. These are not hard and fast rules, and every child is different; you know best when you can trust your kids with hot pans and sharp knives. You'll be amazed at how quickly they learn their way around the kitchen—start them off tearing lettuce leaves and mashing bananas and they'll soon be chopping and sautéing like pros. Hey, you never know, maybe they'll even surprise you with breakfast in bed!

PRESCHOOL CHILDREN: Before they go off to school, kids love spending time with their moms, dads, and grandparents in the kitchen. At this inquisitive age, children are eager to help out, but their hand-eye coordination still needs fine-tuning so it's important to find tasks that are developmentally appropriate. They can:

- help you grocery shop
- wash produce
- pour measured wet and dry ingredients into mixing bowls
- mash and "smash" soft foods
- tear up lettuce and other greens
- toss salads
- participate in taste tests—have your kids rate new dishes using colored star stickers

ELEMENTARY-SCHOOL CHILDREN: When Jesse was in second grade, I organized a "Cooking Idol" birthday party, themed around that year's *American Idol* season finale. The kids divided into groups, and each group made an entrée and a dessert. The menu was simple: Peanut Butter Spaghetti (made with whole wheat pasta, of course) followed by low-fat Chocolate Mousse topped with fresh strawberries. I had pre-measured and prepped all the ingredients in advance, and they had a ball assembling the dishes. A team of parents judged the entries based on presentation and taste and handed out awards. Afterward, we devoured the mouthwatering creations while

American Idol hits blasted in the background, and all the kids went home with aprons and printed copies of the recipes as party favors. The party was a major hit!

During their elementary-school years children develop a better grasp of time sequencing, so they can now follow the steps in a simple recipe from start to finish, as Jesse's friends did at her birthday celebration. They are also beginning to understand fractions and volume amounts, and can now measure out ingredients and mix them together in a bowl. So in a sense, cooking at home builds upon the concepts they're learning in the classroom.

By this time, the kids can:

- use measuring cups and spoons
- learn how to measure accurately
- follow a simple recipe
- mix up the ingredients for meatloaf, meatballs, and burgers
- mix cookie and cake batters
- spoon batter onto baking sheets
- learn to set timers
- use blenders (with close supervision)
- plan simple meals

MIDDLE-SCHOOL CHILDREN: Thanks to the success of programs like *Top Chef* and popular Food Network stars, cooking has become totally cool in the eyes of adolescents. My son, Cole, has quite a few friends who like to experiment with him in the kitchen. The boys have a blast inventing new snack concoctions with whatever they can dig up in the fridge—their latest creation is volcanic cheesy nachos zapped in the microwave and doused with hot sauce. The kitchen may look like a twister tore through it when they're finished, but it's a mess worth making. I love any activity that keeps my kids busy and out of trouble—and distracts them from the computer and TV for a while!

Kids in this age group are able to:

- follow a full, advanced recipe
- measure wet and dry ingredients easily
- break and scramble eggs
- grate cheese and vegetables
- juice and zest citrus fruits
- use food processors and standard and immersion blenders
- use the oven and stovetop (with close supervision)

HIGH-SCHOOL STUDENTS: At this age, kids have much more freedom to make their own food choices, and eating out with friends has become a regular part of their social life. Because they'll undoubtedly eat healthier (and for less $$) at home, it's now more important than ever to get them feeling comfortable and confident in the kitchen. Just make sure you stick around to supervise until you're 100% sure they can handle advanced jobs on their own. Experienced young adults can do just about anything, including:

- develop good knife skills
- chop and grate
- sauté, bake, broil, roast, and grill (indoor/outdoor)
- experiment with new ingredients and cuisines
- browse the web for new recipes to try
- plan and make dinner for the family

Go On, Get Cooking!

With so many good reasons to make healthy home-cooked meals a part of your everyday routine, I imagine you're itching to get started. On the pages that follow, you'll find a collection of scrumptious, no-fuss dishes that I hope will soon be in high demand at your dinner table. My goal was to put together a great all-purpose cookbook, so I've included recipes for breakfast and brunch, soups and salads, stews, chilis, and burgers, and dozens of entrées sorted by category, along with quick veggie side dishes and a delightful assortment of snacks and sweets. Naturally, having experienced the deliciousness of each and every dish, I want you to try them all. But if you're having trouble deciding where to start, dive in with one of my family's top-rated recipes: Spicy Shrimp Jambalaya, Chicken Lettuce Wraps, Buffalo Chicken Chili, Cinnamon-Sugar Almonds, or my favorite decadent *un*splurge, Strawberry Shortcakes with Sweetened Ricotta. If it's kids you aim to please, delight them with a plate of Upside-Down Pan Pizza or AJ's Mac-n-Cheezy (so much better than the box!), finished off with a couple of Soft-Baked Chocolate-Cherry Oatmeal Cookies for dessert. And those dishes are just a sampling of what this book has to offer. Every one of the seventy-five-plus recipes is like a little gift you can share with your loved ones—good, solid nutrition wrapped up in mouthwatering taste and delivered to the table with satisfaction and ease. Unwrap and enjoy!

BREAKFAST & BRUNCH

STRAWBERRY SHORTCAKES
WITH SWEETENED RICOTTA

These pancakes are nothing short of pure, heavenly indulgence! Amazingly, they make for a 100% nutritionally sound breakfast, too. This adorable recipe is a healthful play on traditional strawberry shortcake, with fluffy buttermilk pancakes replacing the fat-laden biscuits and sweetened part-skim ricotta standing in for whipped heavy cream. Sliced fresh strawberries add a good shot of vitamin C and fiber, and the ricotta contributes protein, a must-have nutrient if you're going after a complete breakfast. While I love the hotcakes all dolled up with the topping, I also use the batter on its own as my standard pancake recipe, and I encourage you to do the same. I don't usually resort to begging, but please, please try this recipe on your family—one bite and you'll be as charmed by these pancakes as I am.

SERVES 6 (SERVING SIZE: 2 PANCAKES WITH TOPPING)

PANCAKES

¾ cup whole wheat flour

¾ cup all-purpose flour

2 tablespoons granulated sugar

1½ teaspoons baking powder

¾ teaspoon baking soda

¼ teaspoon kosher salt

2 egg whites

1¾ cups nonfat or low-fat buttermilk

1 tablespoon canola oil

½ teaspoon vanilla extract

TOPPINGS

1 (15-ounce) container part-skim ricotta

2 tablespoons skim milk

6 tablespoons powdered or granulated sugar

½ teaspoon vanilla extract

1 (16-ounce) container fresh strawberries, stemmed and sliced

1   In a large mixing bowl, whisk together the flours, sugar, baking powder, baking soda, and salt until combined.

2   In a medium bowl, lightly beat the egg whites. Add the buttermilk, oil, and vanilla extract and whisk until combined.

3   Pour the wet ingredients over the dry ingredients and stir together gently until just combined, taking care not to overmix. If time allows, let the batter rest for 10 minutes.

4   Liberally coat a large skillet or griddle with oil spray. Preheat it over medium heat. When the pan is nice and hot (after about 2 minutes), ladle about ¼ cup batter per pancake onto the surface. The batter will be thick, so it may help to spread it out with the back of a spoon.

5   Cook the pancakes until they are golden brown, 1 to 2 minutes per side. Recoat the skillet with oil spray between batches to prevent the pancakes from sticking.

6   While the pancakes are cooking, prepare the sweetened ricotta: In a medium mixing bowl, whisk together the ricotta, milk, sugar, and vanilla until smooth.

7   To serve, place 1 pancake in the center of a plate. Spread it with a thin layer of sweetened ricotta (about 2 rounded teaspoonfuls) and a few strawberry slices. Top with a second pancake and spread with another thin layer of sweetened ricotta. Garnish with more sliced berries.

Nutrition Information	Calories – 297 • Protein – 15g • Carbohydrate – 44g • Total fat – 8g
	Saturated fat – 4g • Cholesterol – 30mg • Fiber – 4g • Sodium – 480mg

EGGS BENEDICT
WITH YELLOW PEPPER HOLLANDAISE

You're not going to believe what goes into my guilt-free version of hollandaise. This sauce is just as seductive as the classic recipe, but contains no eggs or butter and doesn't require a culinary degree to pull off. Believe it or not, I use a microwave-steamed yellow bell pepper mixed with low-fat cream cheese to mimic the real thing. The pepper lends the sauce color and lovely flavor, and the cream cheese provides smoothness and texture. Keeping with tradition, I use poached eggs and heart-smart Canadian bacon, and, no surprise, I call for whole grain English muffins. Try this dish for brunch on a lazy Sunday morning. It may be a tad fussy, but you will be glad you made the effort.

SERVES 4

HOLLANDAISE

1 large yellow bell pepper, seeded and cut into eighths

3 ounces (6 tablespoons) reduced-fat cream cheese

1 teaspoon lemon juice

½ teaspoon Dijon mustard

¼ teaspoon kosher salt

EGGS BENEDICT

4 slices Canadian bacon

2 medium ripe tomatoes, each cut into 4 thick slices

4 large eggs, at room temperature

1 teaspoon distilled white vinegar

4 whole grain English muffins, halved

Paprika, for sprinkling

1   Prepare the hollandaise: Place the bell pepper pieces in a microwave-safe bowl, and add 1 tablespoon water. Cover and microwave on high power for 2 minutes, or until the pepper is easily pierced with a paring knife. Drain, and immediately transfer it to a blender.

2   Add the cream cheese, lemon juice, mustard, and salt to the blender. Puree until the sauce is silky smooth with no visible bits of yellow pepper. Set it aside.

3   Prepare the Eggs Benedict: Preheat the broiler. Line a large baking sheet with aluminum foil and coat it with oil spray.

4   Arrange the Canadian bacon and tomato slices in a single layer on the prepared baking sheet. Broil 4 minutes on the first side. Flip the bacon and tomato slices over, and broil for an additional 4 minutes, or until the bacon is crispy brown around the edges. Remove the baking sheet from the oven and loosely tent it with foil to keep it warm.

5   Place a double layer of paper towels on a large platter or small baking sheet; this will be used to hold the poached eggs once they are cooked.

6   Fill a large, shallow pan with 3 inches of water. Bring the water to a boil; then reduce the heat to low (the water should be at a gentle simmer). Add the vinegar to the water.

7   Crack each egg into its own small saucer, ramekin, or bowl. (For the best results, use a container with a narrow base and a wide top to help the egg keep its shape; a small teacup works well.) Place all the cups of egg in close proximity to the stove.

8   Working with 1 egg at a time, slip the eggs carefully into the simmering water by lowering the lip of the cup half an inch below the surface of the water.

9   With a slotted spoon, gently nudge the egg whites closer to the egg yolks by swirling the water around them in a circle as they cook. For medium-firm yolks, cook the eggs for 3 minutes (adjust the time for runnier or firmer yolks, cooking no more than 5 minutes total). To tell if the yolk is cooked to your liking, remove an egg from the water with a slotted spoon and gently press on the yolk to determine the degree of doneness. Remove the cooked eggs from the water with a slotted spoon and transfer them to the paper towel–lined platter.

10 Lightly toast the English muffin halves.

11 Just before serving, reheat the hollandaise in a small saucepan over medium-low heat for a few minutes, or in the microwave for 30 to 60 seconds, until it's warm to the touch.

12 For each serving, place a slice of Canadian bacon on the bottom English muffin half, and pile 2 tomato slices on top. Top with a poached egg and up to ¼ cup of the hollandaise. Sprinkle paprika over the hollandaise. Serve with the top English muffin half alongside.

Nutrition Information	Calories – 295 • Protein – 19g • Carbohydrate – 32g • Total fat – 11g
	Saturated fat – 4g • Cholesterol – 235mg • Fiber – 4g • Sodium – 815mg

DOUBLE CHOCOLATE PANCAKES
WITH STRAWBERRY SAUCE

When the weekend rolls around, these are pretty popular at our house. My kids even brag to their friends that their mom, the nutritionist, makes chocolate pancakes for breakfast. And why not? These are absolutely delicious, with a one-two chocolate punch supplied by cocoa powder and semisweet chocolate chips. Both are sources of flavanols, potent compounds that keep our blood vessels healthy, happy, and flexible. I'm also crafty enough to incorporate both whole wheat flour and flaxseed, which make these flapjacks far superior to your standard pancake mix (don't tell your kids!). Top them with a drop of warm maple syrup or my vitamin C–rich, super-simple strawberry sauce. You get chocolate for breakfast and 6 grams of fiber to boot!

SERVES 6 (SERVING SIZE: 2 PANCAKES WITH TOPPING)

STRAWBERRY SAUCE

1 (16-ounce) package frozen unsweetened whole strawberries

1 tablespoon pure maple syrup

PANCAKES

½ cup whole wheat flour

½ cup all-purpose flour

¼ cup unsweetened cocoa powder

¼ cup granulated sugar

2 tablespoons ground flaxseed

1½ teaspoons baking powder

½ teaspoon kosher salt

1 egg

1 egg white

1 cup skim milk

1 tablespoon canola oil

1 teaspoon vanilla extract

½ cup semisweet chocolate chips

1   Prepare the strawberry sauce: In a large saucepan, combine the frozen strawberries, maple syrup, and 2 tablespoons water. Bring the mixture to a boil. Then reduce the heat to medium-low and simmer for 10 to 15 minutes, or until the sauce reaches a syrupy consistency and coats the back of a spoon. As the sauce simmers, break up the whole berries with a wooden spoon or fork.

2   While the sauce is simmering, prepare the pancake batter: In a large mixing bowl, whisk together the flours, cocoa, sugar, flaxseed, baking powder, and salt.

3   In a medium bowl, lightly beat the whole egg and egg white. Then add the milk, oil, and vanilla, and whisk until combined.

4   Pour the wet ingredients over the dry ingredients and stir until the batter is just blended and no dry streaks remain. Take care not to overmix, as this will cause the pancakes to be chewy. Delicately fold in the chocolate chips. If time allows, let the batter rest for 10 minutes.

5   When the strawberry sauce has reached a syrupy consistency, remove the pan from the heat.

6   Liberally coat a large skillet or griddle with oil spray. Preheat it over medium heat. When the pan is nice and hot (after about 2 minutes), ladle about ¼ cup batter per pancake onto the surface.

7   Cook the pancakes until small bubbles form around the edges, 1 to 2 minutes. Flip the pancakes over and cook about 1 minute longer, until the center is cooked. Recoat the skillet with oil spray between batches to prevent the pancakes from sticking.

8   To serve, top 2 pancakes with about ⅓ cup warm strawberry sauce and a sprinkling of chocolate chips on each plate.

Nutrition Information for 2 pancakes	Calories – 242 • Protein – 7g • Carbohydrate – 38g Total fat – 9g • Saturated fat – 3g • Cholesterol – 35mg Fiber – 4g • Sodium – 260mg
Nutrition Information for ⅓ cup strawberry sauce	Calories – 35 • Protein – 0g Carbohydrate – 9g • Total fat – 0g Saturated fat – 0g • Cholesterol – 0mg Fiber – 2g • Sodium – 0mg

PUMPKIN PANCAKES
WITH MAPLE CRÈME

I'm always looking for ways to jazz up standard pancake batter, and so it was only a matter of time before I perfected a pumpkin version. Plain pureed canned pumpkin is a superhero. It's 100% pure nutrition, packed with potassium and fiber. Plus, it fluffs up the volume of these griddle cakes, already nice and light because of the impressive leavening action of the yogurt reacting with the baking soda. To really push these fabulous flapjacks over the edge, I drizzle on a heavenly blend of reduced-fat cream cheese and maple syrup, then sprinkle with buttery, rich—not to mention nutrient-packed—toasted pecans. This decadent breakfast is sure to impress!

SERVES 6 (SERVING SIZE: 2 PANCAKES WITH TOPPINGS)

PANCAKES

½ cup whole wheat flour

½ cup all-purpose flour

¾ teaspoon baking soda

¼ teaspoon kosher salt

1 tablespoon ground cinnamon

1 teaspoon ground nutmeg

3 egg whites

¾ cup canned 100% pure pumpkin puree

¾ cup nonfat plain yogurt

2 tablespoons packed brown sugar

2 teaspoons vanilla extract

MAPLE CRÈME

4 ounces (½ cup) reduced-fat cream cheese, at room temperature

¼ cup pure maple syrup

TOPPING

¾ cup pecans, toasted (see Note) and roughly chopped

1   In a large mixing bowl, whisk together the flours, baking soda, salt, cinnamon, and nutmeg until well combined.

2   In a second large mixing bowl, whip the egg whites until blended. Add the pumpkin, yogurt, brown sugar, and vanilla extract, and whisk until combined.

3　Pour the wet ingredients over the dry ingredients and stir together gently until just combined and smooth (no dry streaks should remain), taking care not to overmix. If time allows, allow the batter to rest for 10 minutes.

4　Liberally coat a large skillet or griddle with oil spray. Preheat it over medium heat. When the pan is nice and hot (after about 2 minutes), ladle about ¼ cup batter per pancake onto the surface. The batter will be thick, so it may help to spread it out with the back of a spoon.

5　Cook the pancakes until they are golden brown, 2 to 3 minutes per side. Recoat the skillet with oil spray between batches to prevent the pancakes from sticking.

6　While the pancakes are cooking, prepare the maple crème: In a small mixing bowl, whisk together the cream cheese and maple syrup until smooth.

7　To serve, place 2 pancakes on each plate and top them with about 2 tablespoons of the maple crème. Sprinkle with about 2 tablespoons of the chopped pecans.

NOTE: To toast pecans, place them in a dry sauté pan over medium heat and toast, stirring or shaking the pan frequently, until they are lightly browned, about 5 minutes. Or, spread the nuts out on a toaster oven tray and toast for 3 to 4 minutes.

Nutrition Information	Calories – 300 • Protein – 9 g • Carbohydrate – 38 g • Total fat – 14 g
	Saturated fat – 3 g • Cholesterol – 10 mg • Fiber – 5 g • Sodium – 375 mg

ITALIAN SUNDAY BRUNCH BAKE

This all-in-one egg bake is the answer to your brunch dreams. It contains all the elements of a traditional breakfast—including eggs, bacon, and potatoes—but is also packed with sautéed veggies and topped with golden brown Parmesan cheese for amazing flavor and a taste of Italy. The Canadian bacon is leaner than other bacon, yet full-flavored, and the vegetables, having been sautéed briefly before they are added to the dish, are tender and sweet. When you pull this scrumptious casserole from the oven, everyone will get an ample serving for less than 300 calories and a great big blast of nutrition, too.

SERVES 4

1 medium onion, diced

1 red bell pepper, seeded and diced

1 pound small red potatoes, scrubbed and cut into ½-inch pieces

2 teaspoons dried Italian herb blend (or substitute 1 teaspoon dried basil plus 1 teaspoon dried oregano)

1 (8- to 10-ounce) package white button mushrooms, trimmed and thinly sliced

6 slices Canadian bacon, cut into ½-inch pieces

4 cups baby spinach leaves

4 whole eggs

8 egg whites

½ cup skim milk

¼ teaspoon black pepper

2 tablespoons grated Parmesan cheese

1   Preheat the oven to 350°F. Coat a 3- to 4-quart ovenproof casserole dish or a 9×13-inch baking dish with oil spray. Set it aside.

2   Liberally coat a large skillet with oil spray and preheat it over medium-high heat.

3   Add the onions to the skillet and cook, adding water, a tablespoon at a time, as necessary to prevent scorching, until they have softened, about 4 minutes.

4   Add the red bell pepper and potato pieces, and cook until the potatoes begin to soften, 6 to 8 minutes.

5   Add the Italian herb blend and stir well.

6   Add the mushrooms and cook until tender, about 3 minutes.

7   Add the Canadian bacon pieces and stir to combine.

8   Reduce the heat to low, add the baby spinach leaves, and stir just until the spinach wilts. Remove the skillet from the heat and let the vegetable mixture cool to room temperature.

9   In a large mixing bowl, beat the whole eggs and egg whites thoroughly with a whisk. Add the nonfat milk and black pepper, and whisk well to combine.

10 Add the cooled vegetable mixture to the egg mixture and stir well to combine. Pour this into the prepared casserole dish and bake for 25 to 30 minutes, or until the eggs are set and the potatoes are cooked through.

11 Sprinkle the Parmesan cheese over the top, place the dish under the broiler, and broil until the top is golden brown, 4 to 5 minutes. Serve hot.

Nutrition Information	Calories – 297 • Protein – 28 g • Carbohydrate – 30 g • Total fat – 8 g
	Saturated fat – 2 g • Cholesterol – 235 mg • Fiber – 5 g • Sodium – 735 mg

APRICOT ALMOND OATS

Something about a bowl of hot oatmeal sends a reassuring message on cold, gray mornings, and this version is rich, creamy, and satisfying without being over-the-top in terms of calories or sweetness. A fiber-packed bowl of slow-cooked steel-cut oats sweetened with dried apricots and flavored with almond extract is the perfect start to any day. Because it's made with steel-cut oats, which are larger than traditional rolled oats, the glycemic index is slightly lower and so there is even less of an impact in terms of spiking blood sugar. Plus, the larger oats have a pleasingly soft texture. On weekday mornings I like to make a big pot that I cover and leave on the back of the stove. My kids and my husband never fail to stop for a bowl on their way out the door.

SERVES 4 (SERVING SIZE: 1 CUP)

1 cup steel-cut oats

15 whole dried apricots, roughly chopped

½ teaspoon kosher salt

2 tablespoons packed brown sugar

1 teaspoon almond extract (or substitute vanilla extract)

1   Bring 4 cups of water to a boil in a large saucepan.

2   Add the oats, chopped apricots, and salt. Reduce the heat to low and cover the pan. Simmer, stirring occasionally, until the oats are soft and creamy, about 30 minutes.

3   Just before serving, stir in the brown sugar and almond extract.

SERVING SUGGESTION: Ladle 1 cup oatmeal into a bowl and pour up to ½ cup skim milk or unsweetened almond milk around the outer edge.

Nutrition Information	Calories – 242 • Protein – 6 g • Carbohydrate – 48 g • Total fat – 3 g
	Saturated fat – 0.5 g • Cholesterol – 0 mg • Fiber – 6 g • Sodium – 265 mg

MAPLE-PUMPKIN OAT MUFFINS

Warm, freshly baked muffins are fantastic for breakfast or brunch. These are especially good in the fall, when we naturally seem to crave the cozy, inviting flavors of pumpkin, maple, cinnamon, and nutmeg. I absolutely love canned pumpkin—you'll find it in my pantry all year long. It's brimming with beta-carotene, fiber, and potassium and lends incredible flavor, color, and moisture to baked goods without adding a lot of calories. I make these muffins with whole wheat pastry flour, which produces an extra-tender crumb, but feel free to substitute standard whole wheat flour if that's what you have on hand. Give your taste buds a treat and celebrate autumn's arrival with these festive, flavor-filled muffins.

SERVES 12 (SERVING SIZE: 1 MUFFIN)

¾ cup whole wheat pastry flour (or substitute whole-wheat flour)

¾ cup all-purpose flour

½ cup quick-cooking oats

¼ cup granulated sugar

2½ teaspoons baking powder

¼ teaspoon baking soda

¼ teaspoon kosher salt

2 teaspoons pumpkin pie spice

1 large egg

2 tablespoons canola oil

⅓ cup pure maple syrup

1 teaspoon vanilla extract

1 cup canned 100% pure pumpkin puree

½ cup skim milk

2 tablespoons raw unsalted pumpkin seeds (or substitute raw or roasted sunflower seed kernels)

1   Preheat the oven to 375°F. Coat a standard 12-cup muffin pan with oil spray. (If you choose to use muffin liners, use foil liners misted with oil spray to prevent the muffins from sticking to the liners.)

2   In a large mixing bowl, whisk together the flours, oats, sugar, baking powder, baking soda, salt, and pumpkin pie spice.

3   In a medium mixing bowl, whisk together the egg, oil, maple syrup, and vanilla. Add the pumpkin and milk, and whisk to combine.

4   Pour the wet ingredients over the dry ingredients, and using a rubber spatula, gently fold the ingredients together until just combined. Don't worry about leaving a few lumps in the batter.

5   Divide the batter evenly among the 12 muffin cups, filling each cup about two-thirds full. Sprinkle the tops of the muffins with the pumpkin seeds.

6   Bake for 18 to 20 minutes, or until an inserted toothpick comes out clean. Cool completely in the muffin pan before handling.

DIRECTIONS FOR FREEZING: Wrap extra muffins individually in aluminum foil or place them in a freezer bag. Freeze for up to 2 months. For the best results, freeze freshly baked muffins as soon as they have cooled to room temperature.

Nutrition Information	Calories – 154 • Protein – 4 g • Carbohydrate – 27 g • Total fat – 4 g
	Saturated fat – 0.5 g • Cholesterol – 15 mg • Fiber – 2 g • Sodium – 125 mg

SOUPS & SALADS

ASIAN NOODLE SOUP

There is something ultimately soothing and satisfying about a bowl of steaming, aromatic soup loaded with slurp-able noodles. This version bursts with the good flavors of ginger, scallions, mushrooms, and garlic, offset by a dash of pungent sesame oil. While you can use practically any vegetables you have on hand for the soup—think carrots, snowpeas, broccoli, cauliflower, green beans—please don't leave out the edamame. These fresh soybeans are nearly a perfect food with complex carbohydrates, soluble fiber, protein, and omega-3 fats, plus their meaty texture appeals to kids and adults alike. Nearly any green—spinach, watercress, cabbage—can stand in for the bok choy, although the Chinese cabbage is not hard to find. I make this with beef broth for its depth of flavor, but for a vegetarian meal, you'll want to substitute vegetable broth. This is a wonderful way to enjoy a little pasta and a lot of volume while controlling calories and fat.

SERVES 4 (SERVING SIZE: 3 CUPS SOUP WITH ¾ CUP PASTA)

6 to 8 ounces whole wheat thin spaghetti (about half a standard box)

8 cups low-fat unsalted or reduced-sodium beef broth (or substitute chicken or vegetable broth)

3 tablespoons reduced-sodium soy sauce

2 teaspoons grated or finely minced fresh ginger

3 cloves garlic, finely minced

2 cups shelled edamame, fresh or frozen

1 (8- to 10-ounce) package cremini (baby bella) mushrooms, trimmed and sliced

1 large red bell pepper, seeded and thinly sliced

8 to 12 ounces bok choy, trimmed and cut into 2-inch pieces

4 scallions (white and green parts), thinly sliced

1 tablespoon Asian sesame oil

1 teaspoon hot chili paste, such as sriracha (or more to taste)

Bean sprouts, for garnish (optional)

1   Bring a large pot of unsalted water to a boil. Add the spaghetti and cook for 10 to 12 minutes, or according to the package instructions.

2　　While the pasta is cooking, combine the broth, soy sauce, ginger, and garlic in another large pot, and bring to a boil.

3　　Add the edamame, mushrooms, bell pepper, bok choy, and scallions to the broth mixture, and return to a boil. Reduce the heat to low and simmer for 3 to 5 minutes, depending on the desired tenderness of the vegetables.

4　　Remove the soup from the heat, and stir in the sesame oil and chili paste.

5　　Drain the spaghetti well.

6　　To serve, divide the spaghetti evenly among four large serving bowls. Divide the broth-veggie mixture evenly among the bowls, and garnish with the bean sprouts if desired.

Nutrition Information	Calories – 344 • Protein – 25 g • Carbohydrate – 45 g • Total fat – 9 g
	Saturated fat – 2 g • Cholesterol – 0 mg • Fiber – 10 g • Sodium – 600 mg

TOFU TOMATO SOUP
WITH PARMESAN TOAST

Tomato soup and a grilled cheese sandwich has to be one of the all-time great comfort meals. This rendition of the soup is rich and smooth enough to satisfy anyone. The velvety texture comes in large part from the silken tofu that's blended in, and if you don't mention it, no one will even know it's there. The tofu also adds protein to an otherwise carb-rich lunch. Another superstar ingredient is the antioxidant-rich canned tomatoes—for this recipe, I opt for fire-roasted tomatoes for a little more flavor "umph." I don't serve the soup with a standard grilled cheese sandwich but instead suggest my toasty Parmesan-crusted bread, which is perfect for dunking. Enjoy a cozy bowl of tomato soup with a serving of Parmesan toast and you'll have gobbled up 5 grams of fiber and a nice amount of protein . . . not too shabby for this feel-good favorite!

SERVES 4 (SERVING SIZE: 2 CUPS SOUP WITH 1 SLICE TOAST)

SOUP

1 medium onion, diced

2 medium carrots, peeled and diced

2 cloves garlic, crushed

3 tablespoons no-salt-added tomato paste

1 (28-ounce) can diced fire-roasted tomatoes

8 ounces silken tofu, drained and cut into large cubes

Kosher salt and black pepper

PARMESAN TOAST

4 slices whole grain bread

4 tablespoons grated Parmesan cheese

Black pepper

1   To prepare the soup, liberally coat a large pot or Dutch oven with oil spray, and preheat it over medium heat.

2   Add the onion, carrots, and garlic and sauté for 5 minutes, adding a tablespoon of water at a time as necessary to prevent scorching.

3   Stir in the tomato paste and cook, stirring constantly, for 1 minute.

4   Add the canned tomatoes and 28 ounces (1 filled tomato can) of water. Bring the soup to a boil, cover the pot, reduce the heat to low, and simmer for 15 minutes.

5   Preheat the oven to 400°F for the Parmesan toasts.

6   Stir in the tofu and simmer, uncovered, for 15 minutes, or until the vegetables are tender.

7   While the soup is simmering, prepare the Parmesan toasts: Place the bread slices on a baking sheet and lightly mist them with oil spray. Bake for 8 to 10 minutes in the preheated oven. Flip the bread over, sprinkle the top of each slice with 1 tablespoon of the Parmesan cheese, and season with black pepper to taste. Bake for another 3 to 5 minutes, or until the cheese is melted and the bread is toasted. Cut each slice into 4 equal triangles. Set aside.

8   Puree the soup, in small batches, in a blender until completely smooth. (Alternatively, use an immersion blender to puree the soup directly in the pot.) Season it with salt and pepper to taste. Serve with the Parmesan toasts.

Nutrition Information	Calories – 231 • Protein – 15 g • Carbohydrate – 34 g • Total fat – 5 g
	Saturated fat –1 g • Cholesterol – 0 mg • Fiber – 5 g • Sodium – 710 mg

BITE-SIZED CHICKEN MEATBALL SOUP

On bone-chilling winter days, a piping-hot bowl of this soup really hits the spot. First I load the pot with seasonings and veggies galore. And for an interesting twist, I use steel-cut oats as my whole grain starch—not the typical barley, rice, or pasta. But the real highlight of this one-pot supper is the adorable little meatballs, which I make from ground chicken, although ground turkey works just as well. Once the rest of the soup has come together, the bite-sized meatballs take a plunge in the hot pot, where they cook up in just minutes. Ladle it up for your family, sit back, and enjoy the chorus of happily satisfied slurpers.

SERVES 4 (SERVING SIZE: 2 CUPS)

1 small onion, cut into quarters

8 ounces ground chicken (at least 90% lean)

¾ teaspoon kosher salt

½ teaspoon black pepper

1 (8- to 10-ounce) package white button mushrooms, trimmed and thinly sliced

2 cloves garlic, minced

1 tablespoon no-salt-added tomato paste

4 cups low-fat unsalted or reduced-sodium chicken broth

½ cup steel-cut oats

1 bay leaf

½ teaspoon dried oregano

½ teaspoon dried thyme

1 (9-ounce) package frozen artichoke hearts, thawed and quartered, or 1 (14-ounce) can artichoke hearts (packed in water), rinsed, drained, and quartered

1 medium yellow summer squash, cubed

1 (6-ounce) package baby spinach, or 1 (10-ounce) box frozen leaf spinach

1   Finely mince one of the onion quarters.

2   In a medium bowl, mix together the chicken, minced onion, ¼ teaspoon of the salt, and ¼ teaspoon of the black pepper. Shape the chicken mixture into 25 to 30 teaspoon-sized meatballs. Cover and refrigerate until ready to use.

3   Dice the remaining three quarters of the onion.

4   Liberally coat a large pot with oil spray, and preheat it over medium heat.

5   Add the diced onion and the mushrooms to the pot and sauté until softened, about 4 minutes.

6   Add the garlic and tomato paste, and cook, stirring constantly, for 1 minute.

7   Add the chicken broth, oats, bay leaf, oregano, thyme, remaining ½ teaspoon salt and ¼ teaspoon black pepper, and the artichokes, and bring to a boil. Reduce the heat to low and simmer, partially covered, for 20 minutes.

8   Add the yellow squash and the chicken meatballs. Return the mixture to a simmer and cook, uncovered, for 5 minutes, or until the meatballs are cooked through.

9   If using fresh spinach, add the spinach in large batches and cook until just wilted. If using frozen spinach, add the spinach and cook until heated through. Remove the bay leaf before serving.

Nutrition Information	Calories – 283 • Protein – 24g • Carbohydrate – 34g • Total fat – 7g
	Saturated fat – 2g • Cholesterol – 45mg • Fiber – 11g • Sodium – 655mg

CREAMY CURRIED CAULIFLOWER SOUP
WITH MELTED SPINACH

This soup is the ultimate comfort food: creamy, soothing, boldly flavored, and filling. The ginger and the turmeric in the curry powder both have anti-inflammatory properties, so they make this a good-for-you soup as well as a good-tasting soup. I also add garbanzo beans, which team with the cauliflower to provide a remarkable amount of fiber (60% of your daily dose per serving!). The spinach is not actually "melted," but sort of wilts in the soup for a splash of color and pleasing texture. This is a wonderful way to cook cauliflower, an inexpensive and underused cruciferous vegetable. The next time it's on sale at the market, take home a head and stir up a pot of this splendid soup.

SERVES 4 (SERVING SIZE: 2 CUPS)

1 medium onion, diced

2 stalks celery, diced

1 carrot, peeled and diced

2 cloves garlic, crushed

2 teaspoons grated or finely minced fresh ginger

2 tablespoons curry powder

1 head cauliflower, cut into florets

Kosher salt

3 cups skim milk

2 ounces (¼ cup) nonfat cream cheese

1 (15-ounce) can chickpeas, preferably low-sodium, rinsed thoroughly and drained

3 cups baby spinach leaves

Black pepper

1 cup cherry or grape tomatoes, sliced in half

1   Liberally coat a large pot with oil spray, and preheat it over medium heat.

2   Add the onion, celery, carrot, garlic, and ginger. Sauté until the onion becomes translucent, about 5 minutes, adding a tablespoon of water at a time as necessary to prevent the mixture from scorching.

3   Add the curry powder, reduce the heat to low, and cook until the vegetables are soft, 5 to 7 minutes.

4   Add the cauliflower florets, ¾ teaspoon salt, and ½ cup of water. Cover the pot with a tight-fitting lid and raise the heat to medium-high. Cook until the cauliflower is tender, 6 to 8 minutes.

5   In a blender, combine the vegetable mixture with the skim milk and cream cheese. Blend until smooth. If the blender is not large enough to accommodate all the ingredients, divide the vegetable mixture, milk, and cream cheese into two roughly equivalent portions and blend in two batches. (Alternatively, use an immersion blender to puree the soup directly in the pot.)

6   Return the pureed soup to the pot and warm it gently over low heat. Add the chickpeas and baby spinach, and stir until the spinach is wilted. Season with salt and black pepper to taste.

7   Ladle the soup into serving bowls, and garnish with the halved cherry tomatoes.

Nutrition Information	Calories – 271 • Protein – 20g • Carbohydrate – 50g • Total fat – 2g
	Saturated fat – 0g • Cholesterol – 5mg • Fiber – 15g • Sodium – 755mg

ROASTED CHICKEN AND RICE SOUP

Whether you're feeling under the weather or on top of your game, this nourishing, feel-good soup will put a smile on your face and a spring in your step. You'll notice that the soup builds upon my recipe for Lemon-Sage Chicken Breasts on page 129. Here, however, I roast the chicken breasts on a bed of aromatic vegetables, which absorb the fabulous flavors of the seasoned poultry. Then I toss the pulled chicken meat and savory vegetables into a giant pot with store-bought broth and cooked rice to pull it all together. It's nearly impossible to find a whole grain version of this classic comfort food, but leave it to me to break with white starch tradition and incorporate nutritious brown rice. By all means, feel free to swap the rice for any other whole grain, such as whole wheat pasta, wild rice, or barley. Don't wait for the winter months to make this one!

SERVES 8 (SERVING SIZE: 2 CUPS)

4 stalks celery, thinly sliced

4 carrots, peeled and diced

1 large onion, diced

4 cloves garlic, minced

4 bone-in chicken breasts, skin and excess fat removed

Kosher salt and black pepper

1 teaspoon dried thyme

16 fresh sage leaves

1 to 2 lemons, thinly sliced

8 cups low-fat unsalted or reduced-sodium chicken broth

3 cups cooked brown rice

1   Preheat the oven to 400°F. Line a rimmed baking sheet with aluminum foil and coat it with oil spray.

2   Mound the celery, carrots, and onion in the center of the prepared baking sheet. Sprinkle the garlic evenly over the veggies.

3   Place the chicken breasts on top of the vegetables, bone side down, flattening out the veggies just enough to create a bed under the chicken.

4   Sprinkle the chicken with ½ teaspoon salt, ¼ teaspoon black pepper, and the thyme. Place 4 sage leaves on top of each breast; then top the sage leaves with the lemon slices (2 to 3 slices per chicken breast, depending on its size).

5   Bake on the middle oven rack for 40 to 50 minutes, until the inside is no longer pink when slit with a knife or the internal temperature reads 160°F.

6   Remove the chicken from the baking sheet and set it aside to cool slightly. Reserve the lemon slices and sage leaves. Carefully scrape all the veggies and juices from the baking sheet into a large pot or Dutch oven. Add the chicken broth and bring the soup to a simmer.

7   When the chicken breasts have cooled enough to handle, debone them and give the meat a rough chop.

8   Add the chopped chicken, 5 or 6 of the cooked lemon slices, 5 or 6 of the cooked sage leaves, and the cooked brown rice to the pot. Simmer for 20 minutes.

9   Season the soup with salt and pepper to taste. Discard the lemon slices and sage leaves before serving.

Nutrition Information	Calories – 268 • Protein – 34 g • Carbohydrate – 25 g • Total fat – 2 g
	Saturated fat – 0.5 g • Cholesterol – 65 mg • Fiber – 3 g • Sodium – 510 mg

CREAM OF BROCCOLI SOUP

One silky-smooth spoonful of this creamy broccoli soup and you'll be hooked. There are far fewer calories and a lot more beneficial fiber in my rendition than in the classic recipe. Best of all, it's a fantastic source of calcium—a single bowlful provides 50% of an adult's calcium needs for a day.

SERVES 4 (SERVING SIZE: 2½ CUPS)

2 large leeks (white and light green parts), finely chopped

2 large stalks celery, finely chopped

2 cloves garlic, minced

4 cups low-fat unsalted or reduced-sodium chicken broth

2 (16-ounce) packages frozen broccoli florets

1 (15-ounce) can cannellini or white beans, preferably low-sodium, thoroughly rinsed and drained

1 teaspoon ground cumin

1 bay leaf

1 (12-ounce) can fat-free evaporated milk

Kosher salt and black pepper

1 Liberally coat a large pot with oil spray, and preheat it over medium heat.

2 Add the leeks and celery and sauté for 6 to 8 minutes or until slightly softened, adding a little water as needed to prevent scorching.

3 Add the garlic and sauté for 1 minute.

4 Add the chicken broth, broccoli, beans, cumin, and bay leaf, and bring to a boil. Then reduce the heat to low and partially cover the pot. Simmer for 20 minutes.

5 Add the evaporated milk and cook for an additional 2 minutes, uncovered.

6   Remove the pot from the heat and allow the soup to cool slightly, about 5 minutes. Remove the bay leaf.

7   Puree the soup, in small batches, in a blender until completely smooth. Season with salt and pepper to taste before serving.

Nutrition Information	Calories – 302 • Protein – 26g • Carbohydrate – 50g • Total fat – 2g
	Saturated fat – 0g • Cholesterol – 0mg • Fiber – 16g • Sodium – 440mg

SICILIAN QUINOA SALAD

Quinoa is a wonder food—if you have not yet discovered this ancient grain, you are in for a treat. While it's considered a grain, it's actually a seed and therefore high in protein while bursting with good, nutty flavor. When you prepare it, the trickiest part is rinsing it in several changes of cold water to remove the seed's bitter-tasting coating, which is a natural protectant against birds and insects. I toss this super-grain with Swiss chard and fennel. Chard is a nutritional powerhouse full of beta-carotene and folate. Fennel, with its slight taste of licorice, is chard's perfect complement. The raisins are sweet and inviting here, giving the salad an added hit of flavor and texture. Finally, the bright, citrusy dressing has a higher ratio of acid to oil than typical vinaigrettes, which keeps the calories down and the flavor up.

SERVES 6 (SERVING SIZE: 1½ CUPS)

SALAD

1¼ cups quinoa

1 small bulb fennel, tough outer layers discarded, diced

1 large yellow bell pepper, seeded and diced

1 large bunch (about 1 pound) Swiss chard, stems removed, leaves roughly chopped

½ cup loosely packed golden raisins

½ cup pine nuts, toasted (see Note)

VINAIGRETTE

¼ cup 100% orange juice

2 tablespoons lemon juice

1 tablespoon Dijon mustard

¼ teaspoon kosher salt

3 tablespoons olive oil

1 Pour the quinoa into a medium saucepan and fill halfway with warm water. Swish the water with your hand for several seconds; then carefully pour off most of the rinse water. Repeat this rinsing procedure two or three times. After the final rinse, pour off as much rinse water as possible, but don't worry if some water remains in the pan.

2 Add 2¼ cups fresh water to the saucepan, place it over medium-high heat, and bring to a boil. Then reduce the heat to low, cover the pan, and simmer until the quinoa appears translucent and the water has been fully absorbed,

about 15 minutes. Remove from the heat and let stand, uncovered, for at least 5 minutes.

3   Liberally coat a large skillet with oil spray, and preheat it over medium heat.

4   Add the fennel and bell pepper, and cook until the pepper just begins to soften, about 3 minutes.

5   Add the chopped chard leaves and ½ cup water. Cover the skillet with a tight-fitting lid and raise the heat to high. Cook for 2 minutes.

6   Remove the lid and stir the chard mixture. Continue to cook, adding another ¼ cup of water if necessary, until the chard has softened and the fennel and yellow peppers are tender-crisp, about 2 minutes.

7   In a large serving bowl, stir together the cooked quinoa, fennel-chard mixture, golden raisins, and toasted pine nuts.

8   Prepare the vinaigrette: In a small bowl, whisk together the orange juice, lemon juice, Dijon mustard, and salt. Slowly whisk in the olive oil.

9   Pour the vinaigrette over the salad, and toss thoroughly to distribute the vinaigrette. Serve at room temperature or chilled.

NOTE: To toast pine nuts, place them in a dry sauté pan over medium heat. Toast, stirring or shaking the pan frequently, until they are a light golden brown, about 5 minutes.

Nutrition Information	Calories – 343 • Protein – 9 g • Carbohydrate – 43 g • Total fat – 17 g
	Saturated fat – 2 g • Cholesterol – 0 mg • Fiber – 6 g • Sodium – 265 mg

PISTACHIO CHICKEN SALAD

I love chicken salad but rarely order it at restaurants because it's usually drowning in full-fat mayo. Instead, I like to make it at home, where I can control the ingredients and also get creative with healthful mix-ins. This version, with its pop of color from the roasted red peppers and crunch from the pistachios, is one of my all-time favorites. I find pistachios work particularly well in this salad. These little nuggets of heart-healthy goodness are busting with unsaturated fats, fiber, and antioxidants. And while chicken salad wouldn't be chicken salad without the mayo, I toss mine with a reduced-fat variety to save calories and fat. If you're looking for a lean, mean twist on this creamy classic, my Pistachio Chicken Salad is just the ticket.

SERVES 4 (SERVING SIZE: 1 CUP)

½ cup reduced-fat mayonnaise

1 tablespoon white wine vinegar

½ teaspoon kosher salt

½ teaspoon black pepper

1¼ pounds boneless, skinless chicken breasts, cooked, cooled, and cubed

½ medium onion, finely diced

2 stalks celery, finely diced

¼ cup finely diced roasted red bell pepper

¼ cup shelled pistachios, roughly chopped (see Note)

1   In a large mixing bowl, combine the mayonnaise, vinegar, salt, and black pepper.

2   Add the cubed chicken, onion, celery, roasted bell pepper, and pistachios, and stir to coat them evenly with the dressing.

NOTE: You can purchase pistachios already shelled, but since I always have a stash of shell-on pistachios on hand for snacking, I use those instead. The job of shelling the nuts usually goes to one of my kids!

VARIATION: Substitute green apple for the roasted red pepper for a new take on Waldorf salad. Core 1 small Granny Smith apple (unpeeled), finely dice it, and toss it with the rest of the ingredients.

Nutrition Information	Calories – 269 • Protein – 32g • Carbohydrate – 10g • Total fat – 12g
	Saturated fat –2g • Cholesterol – 95mg • Fiber –2g • Sodium – 695mg

PARM AND PEPPER EGG WHITE SALAD

You may be familiar with an Italian classic called *cacio e pepe*. It's a pasta dish flavored with grated Parmesan cheese and lots of freshly ground black pepper. I loosely translated that to create a colorful egg white salad that is terrific served with peppery arugula on whole wheat English muffins or pita bread. The salad is fabulous mixed with shredded lettuce to bump up the volume, which is how I usually enjoy it. The traditional pasta dish does not include vegetables, but since I nixed the pasta, I thought it only right to add the sorts of veggies you'd find in a more typical egg salad. With only 160 calories per serving, this protein-packed lunch will keep you feeling energized for hours.

SERVES 4 (SERVING SIZE: 1¼ CUPS)

¾ cup reduced-fat mayonnaise

½ cup finely grated Parmesan cheese

1 teaspoon freshly ground black pepper (see Notes)

12 large eggs, hard-boiled (see Notes), cooled, yolks removed, whites roughly chopped

½ large red bell pepper, seeded and finely diced

2 medium stalks celery, finely diced

1 In a large mixing bowl, combine the mayonnaise, Parmesan cheese, and black pepper. The dressing will be thick.

2 Add the chopped egg whites, bell pepper, and celery, and stir to evenly coat with the dressing.

NOTES: If you prefer less black pepper, start with only ½ teaspoon and increase to taste.

To make perfect hard-boiled eggs: Place the eggs in a large pot and cover with cold water by at least 1 inch. Bring the water to a rolling boil over medium-high heat. Once the water boils, remove the pot from the heat, cover it with a tight-fitting lid, and let it stand for 15 minutes. Rinse the eggs under cold water until cool to the touch, and they're ready to peel.

Nutrition Information	Calories – 162 • Protein – 15 g • Carbohydrate – 10 g • Total fat – 9 g
	Saturated fat – 2 g • Cholesterol – 5 mg • Fiber – 1 g • Sodium – 705 mg

HEARTY STEWS, CHILIS & BURGERS

WHITE CHILI FIESTA

Once you've made chicken chili, I promise you won't miss the kind made with high-fat beef. This version is full-bodied, easy, and inexpensive. Best of all, it's absolutely packed with beans, which deliver a ferocious amount of fiber—in fact, one bowl of this chili supplies more than 50% of the daily requirement (pretty darn impressive!). Beans are also a great source of protein, iron, and magnesium . . . I really can't praise them enough. I like to pull out this recipe on laid-back nights when I'm in the mood for something smooth, mellow, creamy, and flavorful. As written, the chili is not terribly spicy, although there is a gentle kick. If you want to turn up the heat, leave the seeds in the jalapeños. Or, tame the dish by leaving out the jalapeños and hot sauce altogether. You're in charge!

SERVES 4 (SERVING SIZE: 2 CUPS)

1 pound ground chicken (at least 90% lean)

1 medium onion, diced

1 medium red bell pepper, seeded and diced

2 jalapeños, seeded and finely minced

1 tablespoon chili powder

1½ teaspoons garlic powder

1 teaspoon ground cumin

1 teaspoon dried oregano

¾ teaspoon kosher salt

2 cups low-fat unsalted or reduced-sodium chicken broth

1 cup skim milk

1 medium zucchini, cubed

1 to 2 teaspoons hot sauce (optional)

2 (15-ounce) cans cannellini, white, or great northern beans, preferably low-sodium, rinsed thoroughly and drained

1   Liberally coat a large pot or Dutch oven with oil spray, and preheat it over medium-high heat.

2   Add the ground chicken and cook for 5 minutes, breaking the meat into small crumbles with a wooden spoon.

3   Add the onion, bell pepper, and jalapeños, and sauté for another 5 minutes.

4 Add the chili powder, garlic powder, cumin, oregano, and salt, and stir to evenly coat the chicken with the seasonings.

5 Add the chicken broth, milk, zucchini, and hot sauce (if using).

6 Measure 1 cup of the beans into a small bowl and mash them with a fork until they form a thick paste. Add the bean paste and the remaining whole beans to the pot, and stir well to combine.

7 Bring the chili to a boil. Then reduce the heat to medium-low and simmer, uncovered, for 30 to 40 minutes.

| Nutrition Information | Calories – 419 • Protein – 39g • Carbohydrate – 49g • Total fat – 9g |
| | Saturated fat – 0g • Cholesterol – 75mg • Fiber – 15g • Sodium – 755mg |

BRAZILIAN SEAFOOD STEW

Brazilians are known for their zest for life, an attitude happily reflected in this adventurous seafood stew. Between the garlic, scallions, cilantro, lime, and spicy red pepper, this dish is like one big fiesta in a bowl. Coconut milk, one of the key ingredients, is often found in spicy cuisines because it tempers the heat and smooths out the flavors. However, it's pretty high in fat and calories, so I use *light* coconut milk and add just enough to provide a hint of sweetness and balance. This action-packed stew is perfect for summer entertaining—I bring the entire pot right to the table, with a deep ladle and wide shallow bowls for serving. Of course, you'll need something to wash it all down with, so mix up a pitcher of the Tropical Sangria on page 214!

SERVES 5 (SERVING SIZE: 2 CUPS)

12 ounces bay scallops

12 ounces shrimp, peeled and deveined

⅓ cup lime juice (about 3 large limes)

½ teaspoon kosher salt

½ teaspoon black pepper

2 cloves garlic, minced

1 medium onion, finely chopped

1 medium green bell pepper, seeded and finely chopped

1 medium red bell pepper, seeded and finely chopped

¼ cup finely chopped scallions (white and green parts)

2 cups chopped ripe tomatoes, preferably plum tomatoes

1 teaspoon crushed red pepper flakes

5 cups unsalted or reduced-sodium fish stock (see Note)

½ cup chopped fresh cilantro

1 bay leaf

1 cup light coconut milk (shake the can well before opening)

1 In a large bowl, combine the scallops, shrimp, lime juice, ¼ teaspoon of the salt, the black pepper, and the garlic. Toss to coat. Cover, and marinate in the refrigerator while you prepare the rest of the soup, about 30 minutes.

2 Liberally coat a large pot with oil spray and preheat it over medium heat.

3   Add the onion, green and red bell peppers, and scallions and sauté for 5 minutes, adding a tablespoon of water at a time as necessary to prevent scorching.

4   Add the tomatoes and crushed red pepper flakes to the pot and cook for 10 minutes, stirring frequently.

5   Add the fish stock, ¼ cup of the cilantro, the bay leaf, and remaining ¼ teaspoon salt. Bring the soup to a boil, reduce the heat to low, and simmer, uncovered, for 10 minutes.

6   Add the coconut milk and the marinated shrimp-scallop mixture (including all liquids) to the pot. Cook over medium heat, stirring occasionally, until the shrimp are fully cooked, about 2 minutes. Remove the bay leaf, and sprinkle the reserved ¼ cup cilantro over the stew before serving.

NOTE: If your store doesn't carry fish stock, you can substitute a mixture of 1 cup bottled clam juice and 4 cups unsalted or reduced-sodium chicken broth.

Nutrition Information	Calories – 238 • Protein – 30g • Carbohydrate – 16g • Total fat – 5g
	Saturated fat – 3g • Cholesterol – 125mg • Fiber – 4g • Sodium – 840mg

ITALIAN CHICKEN AND SAUSAGE STEW

Although this is sort of a mutt of a stew—with the flavors of southern Italy and those of Louisiana vying for prominence—it's sure to get rave reviews from anyone lucky enough to be invited to dinner. I use Italian-style poultry sausage for a taste of Italy and rely on okra to send the taste buds down home to the bayou. The tomatoes, peppers, and garlic cross international boundaries and work to pull the sausage and chicken together into a full-bodied dish your palate will love. Okra is a good source of fiber and folate, and rest assured: any sliminess is well masked in this stew (I suggest buying frozen okra for ease). This hearty one-pot wonder makes a delish meal any night of the week, but it is particularly perfect for those times when you're feeding a crowd.

SERVES 6 (SERVING SIZE: 2 CUPS)

1½ pounds boneless, skinless chicken breasts, cut into 1-inch pieces

1 medium onion, diced

3 stalks celery, diced

1 red bell pepper, seeded and diced

3 cloves garlic, minced

1 (28-ounce) can no-salt-added diced tomatoes

2 cups chopped okra (fresh or frozen)

2½ cups cut green beans (fresh or frozen)

3 links spicy Italian-style chicken or turkey sausage, fully cooked and sliced into rounds

2 teaspoons dried basil

2 teaspoons dried oregano

½ teaspoon dried thyme

¼ teaspoon fennel seeds, crushed

½ teaspoon kosher salt

¼ teaspoon black pepper

1   Liberally coat a large pot or Dutch oven with oil spray, and preheat it over medium heat.

2   Add the chicken and sauté for about 6 minutes, or until it is cooked through and lightly browned. Transfer the chicken to a plate.

3   Return the pot to medium heat and reapply oil spray, liberally coating the bottom of the pot.

4   Add the onion, celery, red bell pepper, and garlic and sauté, stirring occasionally, until tender, about 10 minutes. Add water, a tablespoon at a time, as necessary to prevent scorching.

5   Add the tomatoes, okra, green beans, sausage, reserved chicken, and seasonings. Bring the stew to a boil. Then reduce the heat to low, cover the pot, and simmer gently for 30 minutes, stirring occasionally to evenly coat everything with the sauce.

Nutrition Information	Calories – 270 • Protein – 37 g • Carbohydrate – 17 g • Total Fat – 6 g
	Saturated Fat – 1 g • Cholesterol – 95 mg • Fiber – 7 g • Sodium – 605 mg

RATATOUILLE LENTIL STEW

When summer's vegetables are at their best, ratatouille is a lovely addition to the table: thick, mellow, soft, and bursting with flavor without bragging. My version features all of the usual suspects—tomato, eggplant, zucchini, and bell peppers—but also introduces nutrient-packed lentils, which turn this traditional side dish into a satisfying main meal. Aside from costing just pennies per serving, lentils offer protein and fiber, a dynamic duo that keeps you feeling full for hours. I roast the vegetables first with a spritz of oil spray to bring out their richest, deepest flavors without adding extra fat and calories. If you're lucky enough to have leftovers, no need to heat it up . . . it's equally good served cold, straight from the fridge.

SERVES 4 (SERVING SIZE: 2½ CUPS)

1 small eggplant, cubed

1 red bell pepper, seeded and cut into ½-inch pieces

1 yellow bell pepper, seeded and cut into ½-inch pieces

1 zucchini, cubed

1 yellow summer squash, cubed

2 teaspoons dried oregano

1 teaspoon crushed dried rosemary

1 medium onion, diced

2 medium carrots, peeled and diced

2 celery stalks, diced

3 cloves garlic, minced

¼ cup no-salt-added tomato paste

1 cup lentils, rinsed

4 cups unsalted or reduced-sodium vegetable broth

¼ to ½ teaspoon kosher salt

Juice of 1 lemon

1 Preheat the oven to 400°F.

2 Divide the eggplant, bell peppers, zucchini, and yellow squash between two large baking sheets, and spread the vegetables out into a single, even layer on each sheet. Coat the vegetables liberally with oil spray, and then sprinkle the oregano and rosemary evenly over them.

3 Roast the vegetables in the oven for 30 to 40 minutes or until tender, stirring them about halfway through.

4   While the vegetables are roasting, prepare the soup base: Liberally coat a large pot with oil spray, and preheat it over medium-high heat.

5   Add the onion, carrots, celery, and garlic to the pot. Sauté for 5 to 7 minutes, or until the vegetables have softened, adding a tablespoon of water at a time as necessary to prevent scorching.

6   Add the tomato paste and cook, stirring, for about 2 minutes.

7   Add the lentils, vegetable broth, 1 cup water, and ¼ teaspoon of the salt. Bring to a boil. Then reduce the heat to low and simmer, covered, for 30 minutes.

8   Add the roasted vegetables to the pot and stir thoroughly to combine. Simmer, covered, for another 10 minutes or until the lentils are tender.

9   Remove the pot from the heat and stir in the lemon juice. Taste for seasoning, and add the remaining ¼ teaspoon salt if desired. To serve, ladle the soup into bowls.

Nutrition Information	Calories – 383 • Protein – 21g • Carbohydrate – 69g • Total Fat – 6g
	Saturated Fat –1g • Cholesterol – 0mg • Fiber – 18g • Sodium – 740mg

BUFFALO CHICKEN CHILI
WITH WHIPPED BLUE CHEESE

Who says you shouldn't indulge in the rich, spicy flavors of Buffalo wings? This chili lets you enjoy all the fun of the original without the fat, calories, and guilt. Rather than cooking chicken wings, with their high ratio of skin to meat, I've turned this party-time favorite into a ground chicken stew you and your family will love and make time and again. Go ahead and use ground turkey if you can't find ground chicken; it's an easy swap. I couldn't believe how sensational this tasted when I made it for the first time: I thought I had died and gone to Buffalo!

SERVES 4 (SERVING SIZE: 2¼ CUPS WITH TOPPING)

CHILI

6 carrots, peeled, halved lengthwise, and sliced into half-moons

6 stalks celery, sliced

6 cloves garlic, minced

2 pounds ground chicken breast (99% lean)

2 tablespoons chili powder

2 tablespoons all-purpose flour

4 cups low-sodium vegetable or tomato juice

¼ to ½ cup hot sauce (see Note)

¼ teaspoon kosher salt

TOPPING

¼ cup nonfat sour cream

¼ cup blue cheese crumbles

1   Liberally coat a large pot or Dutch oven with oil spray, and preheat it over medium-high heat.

2   Add the carrots and celery and sauté, stirring occasionally, until tender, about 10 minutes; add water, a tablespoon at a time, as necessary to prevent scorching.

3   Add the garlic and sauté for 1 minute.

4   Add the ground chicken, reapplying oil spray if necessary. Sauté, stirring continuously and breaking the chicken into small pieces, for 5 minutes or until cooked through. As the chicken cooks, continue scraping the bottom of the pan with a wooden spoon to dislodge any large bits.

5   Sprinkle in the chili powder and flour, and stir quickly to distribute them evenly. Immediately add the vegetable juice and hot sauce, and bring to a boil. Reduce the heat to low and simmer, partially covered, stirring occasionally, for about 20 minutes.

6   While the chili is simmering, prepare the blue cheese topping: In a small bowl, mash together the sour cream and blue cheese with a fork until well combined. Set aside.

7   Season the chili with the salt. Ladle the chili into serving bowls and top each with about 2 tablespoons of the blue cheese topping.

NOTE: The amount of hot sauce you use will depend on the brand you select as well as your (and your family's) own personal tolerance for spicy foods. I advise adding ¼ cup hot sauce to start with, then tasting the chili and adding more from there if you find it too mild.

Nutrition Information	Calories – 369 • Protein – 53 g • Carbohydrate – 33 g • Total fat – 4 g
	Saturated fat – 1 g • Cholesterol – 135 mg • Fiber – 7 g • Sodium – 665 mg

TANDOORI CHICKEN BURGERS
WITH CARROT RAITA

This is one of the easiest burger recipes ever—and in my opinion, one of the best tasting, too. I am endlessly intrigued by Indian cuisine, and so for this recipe I worked classic Indian seasonings into a burger that wound up tasting as if it had been cooked in a traditional tandoori oven. As the burgers cook, they fill the kitchen with amazing aromas that make everyone eager for dinner. The raita topping, made with nonfat yogurt and shredded carrot, cools down the spice and adds its own flavor dimension. And this burger recipe is a good way to get a dose of turmeric, truly a wonder spice in terms of its anti-inflammatory properties. No need for a bun—this perfectly seasoned burger is a star on its own!

SERVES 4 (SERVING SIZE: 1 BURGER WITH TOPPING)

CARROT RAITA

1 medium carrot, peeled and grated

½ cup nonfat plain yogurt

1 clove garlic, finely minced

Juice of ½ lemon

1 teaspoon chopped fresh mint (optional)

BURGERS

Juice of ½ lemon

1 teaspoon ground cumin

1 teaspoon ground turmeric

1 teaspoon paprika

½ teaspoon garlic powder

½ teaspoon ground coriander

½ teaspoon cayenne pepper

¼ teaspoon kosher salt

1 pound ground chicken (at least 90% lean; or substitute ground turkey)

4 cups shredded lettuce

1 In a small bowl, mix together the grated carrot, yogurt, garlic, lemon juice, and mint if using. Let the raita sit at room temperature while you prepare the burgers.

2 Preheat an outdoor grill, indoor grill pan, or large skillet over medium-high heat. Liberally coat the cooking surface with oil spray.

3   In a large bowl, whisk together the lemon juice and all the seasonings. Add the ground chicken and mix thoroughly until the seasonings are evenly distributed. Form the chicken mixture into 4 patties.

4   Place the burgers on the grill or skillet, and cook for 5 minutes on the first side.

5   Mist the top of the burgers lightly with oil spray (to prevent sticking on the second side), and then flip them over. Cook for 3 to 5 minutes, or until they are no longer pink in the center.

6   Top each burger with shredded lettuce and a spoonful (about 2 tablespoons) of the carrot raita.

Nutrition Information	Calories – 211 • Protein – 30 g • Carbohydrate – 9 g • Total fat – 7 g
	Saturated fat – 2 g • Cholesterol – 100 mg • Fiber – 2 g • Sodium – 250 mg

GARDEN LENTIL BURGERS

These burgers are packed with good-for-you vegetables, which make them extra-flavorful and incredibly nutrient-dense, and the water chestnuts give them a satisfying crunch. The lentils are a good source of protein, and coupled with the brown rice, provide excellent fiber. While it takes some effort to prepare them, the burgers freeze beautifully. I highly recommend doubling the recipe and making enough to freeze for later in the month—they're great to have on hand when you need to put dinner on the table in a flash. Make tonight vegetarian night!

SERVES 8 (SERVING SIZE: 1 BURGER)

1 tablespoon canola oil

1 medium onion, finely diced

2 cloves garlic, minced

1 medium carrot, peeled and grated

1 medium zucchini, grated

1 cup cooked brown lentils

1½ cups cooked brown rice, preferably short-grain

½ cup finely diced roasted red peppers

1 (8-ounce) can water chestnuts, drained and finely diced

1 teaspoon dried thyme

1 tablespoon Dijon mustard

1 tablespoon reduced-sodium soy sauce

½ teaspoon kosher salt

2 large egg whites, beaten

1 cup unseasoned whole wheat bread crumbs

1   Heat the canola oil in a large sauté pan over medium heat.

2   Add the onion and garlic and cook until the onion is translucent and beginning to soften, about 3 minutes.

3   Add the carrot and zucchini, and sauté for 3 to 4 minutes, until the vegetables are tender. Let the vegetable mixture cool to room temperature.

4   In a large mixing bowl, combine the cooked lentils, cooked rice, cooked vegetables, roasted red peppers, water chestnuts, thyme, Dijon mustard, soy sauce, and salt.

5   Fold the egg whites into the lentil mixture, and mix thoroughly until all the ingredients are evenly distributed.

6   Stir in the bread crumbs, a handful at a time, until the mixture resembles a traditional meatloaf in texture and holds together when compacted into a ball. (You may not need the full cup of bread crumbs.)

7   Form the mixture into 8 patties (about ⅔ cup mixture per patty), firmly packing each patty.

8   Liberally coat a large skillet or sauté pan with oil spray, and preheat it over medium heat.

9   Working in batches, cook the patties on one side until they are golden brown, about 5 minutes.

10 Carefully flip the patties over and cook until the second side is browned, 4 to 5 minutes. Take care when flipping the patties, as they will be delicate. Recoat the pan with oil spray between batches to prevent the patties from sticking.

Directions for freezing: Cook the patties as directed, and then let them cool completely. Wrap each patty individually in plastic wrap, place them in a plastic freezer bag, and store in the freezer for up to 2 months. To reheat, simply microwave from the frozen state for about 2 minutes, or until heated through.

Nutrition Information	Calories – 191 • Protein – 7 g • Carbohydrate – 37 g • Total fat – 3 g
	Saturated fat – 0 g • Cholesterol – 0 mg • Fiber – 5 g • Sodium – 295 mg

PASTA ENTRÉES

AJ'S MAC-N-CHEEZY

When I started work on this book, I promised my youngest, Ayden Jane, that I would come up with a recipe for macaroni and cheese that met her approval, and that when I did I would name it for her. Here it is: AJ's Mac-n-Cheezy, kid-tested and approved with a five-star rating! In the interest of full disclosure, it took *several* attempts (dozens, really) before I mastered a version that earned Ayden's two thumbs up. But Ayden's persistence paid off, and the entire Bauer brood agrees that this mac and cheese is to die for. This creamy, irresistible childhood favorite provides 75% of your daily requirement for calcium and far fewer calories and fat than traditional recipes.

SERVES 6 (SERVING SIZE: 1½ CUPS)

1 (10-ounce) block (or 2½ cups pre-shredded) 2% reduced-fat sharp cheddar cheese (see Note)

1 (14- to 16-ounce) box whole wheat elbow macaroni

2¼ cups cold skim or 1% milk

1 teaspoon low-sodium soy sauce

1 teaspoon onion powder

½ teaspoon dry mustard

¼ teaspoon paprika

1 bay leaf

½ teaspoon kosher salt

⅛ teaspoon black pepper

3 to 5 drops hot sauce

1 tablespoon cornstarch

2 tablespoons trans-fat-free reduced-fat soft tub margarine spread

1   If using block cheese, shred the cheese using the large side of a box grater, and set it aside to warm to room temperature. (Having the cheese closer to room temperature helps it to melt more easily.) If using pre-shredded cheese, remove the bag(s) from the fridge and set them on the counter to warm to room temperature.

2   Bring a large pot of unsalted water to a boil. Add the macaroni and follow the directions on the package for al dente pasta.

3   While the macaroni is cooking, prepare the cheese sauce: In a large saucepan, combine 2 cups of the milk with the soy sauce, onion powder, dry mustard, paprika, bay leaf, salt, black pepper, and hot sauce. Place over medium heat, and cook until the mixture comes to a gentle simmer.

4   In a small bowl or cup, mix the cornstarch with the remaining ¼ cup cold milk. Add the cornstarch mixture to the sauce and stir to combine. Return the sauce to a simmer and cook for 2 to 3 minutes, stirring occasionally. The mixture should thicken slightly.

5   Remove the saucepan from the heat, discard the bay leaf, and add the shredded cheese. Continue stirring until the cheese is completely melted and no lumps remain.

6   Add the margarine spread to the cheese sauce and stir until it is completely melted and combined.

7   Drain the macaroni (do not rinse it), and return it to the pot.

8   Pour the cheese sauce over the cooked macaroni and stir until everything is coated. Cover the pot with a tight-fitting lid and allow the macaroni and cheese to sit for 5 to 10 minutes, to allow the sauce to thicken before serving.

NOTE: To produce a creamy final product, make sure you use cheese made with 2% milk, not 1.5% or 1% milk.

VARIATION: For baked macaroni and cheese with a crispy, crunchy top: After combining the cheese sauce with the cooked macaroni, transfer the mixture to a 9×13-inch baking dish coated with oil spray. Sprinkle it with ¼ cup shredded or grated Parmesan cheese. Place under a preheated broiler for 4 to 7 minutes, or until the top is golden brown and crispy; check often to make sure the cheese does not burn.

Nutrition Information	Calories – 419 • Protein – 25 g • Carbohydrate – 58 g • Total fat – 13 g
	Saturated fat – 6 g • Cholesterol – 35 mg • Fiber – 6 g • Sodium – 680 mg

TURKEY TETRAZZINI

When it came to creating a leaner version of this conventionally rich, high-calorie dish made with pasta, turkey, and a creamy cheese sauce, I definitely had my work cut out for me. But after fussing with quite a few "first drafts" that didn't make the cut, I'm happy to say I nailed this final recipe. My turkey tetrazzini has about half the calories and fat of the traditional dish but is still packed with flavor, thanks to the artichoke hearts, roasted red peppers, and mushrooms as well as the Parmesan cheese. Low-fat cream cheese provides all the creaminess you could want and makes every bite soulfully satisfying. This recipe is a little more complex than others in the book, but don't let that deter you for a single minute—once you've added it to your repertoire, it's destined to become a family favorite!

SERVES 6 (SERVING SIZE: 1½ CUPS)

1 pound turkey breast cutlets (or substitute boneless, skinless chicken breasts or chicken tenders)

½ teaspoon kosher salt

¾ teaspoon black pepper

1 medium onion, diced

1 (8- to 10-ounce) package white button mushrooms, trimmed and sliced

3 cloves garlic, minced

¼ teaspoon crushed red pepper flakes

⅓ cup all-purpose or whole wheat flour

3 cups low-fat unsalted or reduced-sodium chicken broth

8 ounces whole wheat pasta (about half a standard box; angel hair, spaghetti, or linguine work best)

4 ounces (½ cup) low-fat cream cheese

½ cup grated Parmesan cheese

1 cup chopped roasted red bell peppers

1 (14-ounce) can artichoke hearts packed in water or brine, thoroughly rinsed and drained, roughly chopped

6 cups fresh spinach, large stems removed, leaves roughly chopped

1 Preheat the oven to 350°F.

2 Bring a large pot of unsalted water to a boil.

3   While the water is heating, liberally coat a second large pot or Dutch oven with oil spray, and preheat it over medium heat.

4   Season the turkey cutlets with ¼ teaspoon of the salt and ¼ teaspoon of the black pepper. Place the cutlets in the pot and cook on the first side until nicely browned, 6 to 8 minutes. Turn the cutlets over and finish cooking on the other side until browned, about 4 minutes. Transfer the cutlets to a plate.

5   In the same pot, liberally reapply oil spray and add the onion. Cook, stirring occasionally, until soft and translucent, about 4 minutes, adding a tablespoon of water at a time as necessary to prevent scorching.

6   Add the mushrooms, garlic, and red pepper flakes. Sauté, stirring occasionally, until the mushrooms are soft, about 5 minutes.

7   Push the vegetables to the outskirts of the pot to create a well in the center. Add the flour to the well. Pour 1 cup of the chicken broth over the flour, whisking vigorously, and continue whisking to combine the flour and broth into a thick paste.

8   Slowly start to bring the vegetables into the paste; then stir to thoroughly combine. Cook for 2 to 3 minutes, stirring occasionally, to allow the raw flour taste to cook out.

9   Add the remaining 2 cups broth and whisk vigorously to combine. Still working over medium heat, bring the sauce to a gentle simmer and cook for about 10 minutes. The sauce will begin to thicken slightly.

10   While the sauce is simmering, break the pasta into 2-inch pieces (roughly) with your hands. Add the pasta pieces to the boiling water and cook until just al dente, about 5 minutes (depending upon the pasta cut). Don't overcook the pasta; it will continue to cook in the oven. Drain the pasta, reserving ½ cup of the cooking water. Set aside.

11   Season the sauce with the remaining ¼ teaspoon salt and ½ teaspoon black pepper. Add the cream cheese and ¼ cup of the Parmesan cheese. Stir until the cream cheese is completely melted and incorporated.

12   Chop the reserved turkey cutlets into ½-inch pieces.

13   Add the chopped turkey, roasted red peppers, artichoke hearts, and spinach to the sauce. Continue stirring until the spinach is wilted, about 1 minute.

14   Add the cooked pasta. Stir until all the ingredients are evenly coated with sauce. If the sauce is too thick, thin it with the reserved pasta water, adding 2 tablespoons at a time and stirring after each addition to test the consistency.

15   Transfer the mixture to a baking dish coated with oil spray, and smooth the top. Or if you used a Dutch oven, simply remove it from the heat and smooth the mixture directly in the dish.

16   Sprinkle the remaining ¼ cup Parmesan cheese evenly over the casserole.

17   Bake, uncovered, on the middle oven rack for 20 to 25 minutes, or until the top is golden and the casserole is bubbling around the sides.

Nutrition Information	Calories – 374 • Protein – 34 g • Carbohydrate – 47 g • Total fat – 7 g
	Saturated fat – 3 g • Cholesterol – 50 mg • Fiber – 7 g • Sodium – 700 mg

CHICKEN FETTUCCINE ALFREDO
WITH SUN-DRIED TOMATOES

Pasta Alfredo doesn't have to be a heart attack on a plate. In fact, my secret recipe is so surprisingly lean that you can enjoy it on a regular basis, rather than as a once-in-a-blue-moon splurge. The creamy sauce is made with fat-free evaporated milk blended with reduced-fat cream cheese, which provides the requisite velvety texture, and finished with Parmesan cheese for a sharp-salty flavor. This is classy enough to serve to guests, but simple enough for a weeknight family dinner. Feel free to skip the sun-dried tomatoes if you'd like a more classic version, but I like them for their pop of color.

SERVES 5 (SERVING SIZE: 2 CUPS)

1¼ pounds boneless, skinless chicken breasts, cut into ½-inch pieces

Kosher salt and black pepper

1 (8- to 10-ounce) package cremini (baby bella) mushrooms, trimmed and sliced

1 (12- to 14-ounce) package whole wheat linguine or fettuccine

1 (12-ounce) can fat-free evaporated milk

3 ounces (6 tablespoons) reduced-fat cream cheese, at room temperature

½ cup grated Parmesan cheese

½ cup "ready-to-eat" sun-dried tomatoes, sliced into thin ribbons (see Notes)

1   Bring a large pot of unsalted water to a boil.

2   While the pasta water is heating, prepare the chicken and mushrooms: Liberally coat a large skillet or sauté pan with oil spray, and preheat it over medium heat.

3   Season the chicken pieces with ¼ teaspoon salt and ¼ teaspoon black pepper. Add them to the skillet and sauté until cooked through,

5 to 7 minutes. Transfer the chicken to a large serving bowl (the bowl should be large enough to accommodate the finished dish).

4   Return the skillet to the stove and raise the heat to medium-high. Reapply oil spray, liberally coating the bottom of the skillet. Add the mushrooms and sauté until they are golden brown, about 5 minutes. Transfer the mushrooms to the serving bowl with the chicken.

5   Drop the pasta into the boiling water and cook according to the package instructions.

6   While the pasta cooks, prepare the Alfredo sauce: In a 2-quart saucepan, combine the evaporated milk, cream cheese, ½ teaspoon salt, and ¼ teaspoon black pepper.

7   Place the saucepan over medium-low heat and cook, stirring occasionally with a wire whisk to break up the cream cheese, until the cream cheese is completely melted and the mixture is barely simmering, 5 to 7 minutes. Be careful not to overheat the mixture because the milk will curdle.

8   Stir in the Parmesan cheese and whisk for 1 minute. Remove the Alfredo sauce from the heat.

9   Drain the pasta, reserving approximately 1 cup of the cooking water.

10 Add the pasta, sliced sun-dried tomatoes, and Alfredo sauce to the chicken and mushrooms, and toss to coat all the ingredients evenly with the sauce. Season with salt and pepper to taste. Serve immediately. (The sauce will begin to thicken as it stands. If you'd like to thin it out as it cools, add the reserved pasta water in ¼-cup increments until the desired consistency is achieved.)

NOTES: For this recipe, you should use sun-dried tomatoes that are not packed in oil. Ready-to-eat sun-dried tomatoes are usually found in plastic tubs or vacuum-sealed packages in the produce section of the grocery store. Ready-to-eat sun-dried tomatoes are pliable and don't require rehydration. If you purchase brittle sun-dried tomatoes, they will need to be rehydrated before use in this recipe: Place the tomatoes in a bowl, add enough hot water to cover, and soak for 20 minutes or until tender.

Because the Alfredo sauce thickens in the fridge, when reheating leftovers, I recommend you add a splash of water to moisten it; then microwave, and stir before serving.

Nutrition Information	Calories – 497 • Protein – 47 g • Carbohydrate – 58 g • Total fat – 8 g
	Saturated fat – 3 g • Cholesterol – 85 mg • Fiber – 8 g • Sodium – 765 mg

SUMMERY PESTO PASTA

Pesto sauce is traditionally super-rich in olive oil, and while olive oil has definitely earned its reputation as a heart-healthy fat, like all other fats, it's incredibly calorie-dense and should be used in moderation. Here I've put together a low-cal sauce that's still as bright and summery-tasting as any pesto this side of the Mediterranean. By sautéing fresh zucchini and tomatoes in a bit of olive oil before tossing them with the pasta and pesto, I incorporate just enough oil to pull it all together. My daughter Jesse, a self-described pesto connoisseur, asks for this dish all summer long, when we have armloads of basil growing in the garden, and I am happy to oblige. This is a great pasta entrée served warm or cold, and if you want to bulk up the meal, add some diced chicken breast or shrimp for protein. Outstanding!

SERVES 4 (SERVING SIZE: 2½ CUPS)

PESTO SAUCE

4 cups loosely packed fresh basil leaves

¼ cup grated Parmesan cheese

3 cloves garlic, quartered

½ cup low-fat unsalted or reduced-sodium chicken broth

1 teaspoon kosher salt

¼ teaspoon black pepper

PASTA AND VEGETABLES

1 (12- to 14-ounce) package whole wheat penne

1 tablespoon olive oil

1 large zucchini, cut into 1-inch wedges

1 pint cherry tomatoes, halved

8 tablespoons grated Parmesan cheese

1   Prepare the pesto: Combine the basil, Parmesan cheese, garlic, chicken broth, salt, and black pepper in a food processor or blender, and process to form a loose paste. Set the pesto sauce aside.

2   Bring a large pot of unsalted water to a boil, and cook the penne according to the package directions.

3   While the pasta cooks, heat the olive oil in a large skillet over medium heat.

4   Add the zucchini to the skillet and sauté until just softened, about 4 minutes.

5   Add the tomatoes and continue to cook the vegetables for another 2 to 3 minutes. Remove from the heat.

6   Drain the penne and return it to the pot.

7   Add the sautéed vegetables and the pesto sauce to the pasta, and toss gently until all the ingredients are evenly coated with the sauce. Top each serving with up to 2 tablespoons of the Parmesan cheese.

Nutrition Information	Calories – 435 • Protein – 22g • Carbohydrate – 73g • Total Fat – 9g
	Saturated fat – 3g • Cholesterol – 10mg • Fiber – 3g • Sodium – 750mg

PASTA WITH TURKEY BOLOGNESE

There are some dishes that I can't outlaw from my repertoire, and pasta with a rich, meaty Bolognese sauce is certainly one. Happily, I've developed a hearty yet guilt-free version that will excite both your taste buds and your cardiologist. To slash the calories and artery-clogging fat (but of course keep the flavor), I rely on turkey bacon and ground turkey. The bacon imparts the necessary smoky undertones, while the ground turkey provides bulk and full flavor. A sprinkling of nutmeg and allspice enhances the richness of this lip-smacking sauce. Instead of stirring in whole milk as your Italian grandma might have done, I finish the sauce with calcium-rich fat-free evaporated milk, which makes it smooth and creamy. Finally, I use only ⅓ cup of red wine, which leaves plenty in the bottle to enjoy with the meal. Now, that's what I call good planning!

SERVES 6 (SERVING SIZE: 1½ CUPS)

2 slices turkey bacon, finely chopped

2 cloves garlic, finely minced

1 large carrot, peeled and finely chopped

2 stalks celery, finely chopped

1 medium onion, finely chopped

1¼ pounds ground turkey (at least 90% lean)

⅓ cup dry red wine

1 cup low-fat unsalted or reduced-sodium beef broth

1 (15-ounce) can no-salt-added diced tomatoes

3 tablespoons no-salt-added tomato paste

½ teaspoon kosher salt

¼ teaspoon black pepper

2 bay leaves

¼ teaspoon ground thyme

⅛ teaspoon ground nutmeg

1 pinch ground allspice

1 (12- to 14-ounce) package whole wheat linguine or spaghetti

⅓ cup fat-free evaporated milk

1   Liberally coat a large pot with oil spray, and preheat it over medium heat.

2   Add the turkey bacon and cook, stirring frequently, for about 1 minute.

3   Add the garlic, carrot, celery, and onion and sauté until the onion is translucent, about 5 minutes, adding a tablespoon of water at a time as necessary to prevent scorching.

4   Raise the heat to medium-high and add the ground turkey, stirring to break up the meat. Cook until the meat is no longer pink, about 5 minutes.

5   Add the wine and simmer until most of the liquid has evaporated.

6   Stir in the broth, tomatoes, tomato paste, and seasonings and bring the sauce to a boil. Then reduce the heat to low and simmer, uncovered, for about 30 minutes, stirring occasionally.

7   While the sauce simmers, bring a large pot of unsalted water to a boil, add the linguine, and cook according to the directions on the package for al dente pasta. Drain well.

8   To finish the sauce, stir in the evaporated milk and cook until just heated through, about 1 minute. Discard the bay leaf.

9   Turn off the heat and add the pasta directly to the sauce. Toss to coat the pasta evenly with the sauce, and serve.

Nutrition Information	Calories – 376 • Protein – 32 g • Carbohydrate – 46 g • Total fat – 5 g
	Saturated fat – 1 g • Cholesterol – 65 mg • Fiber – 8 g • Sodium – 375 mg

HALIBUT AND ROTINI
WITH SPRING PEA PUREE

Looking for an impressive meal to serve to company? You've arrived at the right recipe! This beautiful dish starts off with a base of delicate pea puree, which is then topped with whole grain rotini tossed with brightly colored tomatoes and tender chunks of fresh halibut. The result is an elegant dish with refined flavor and a gourmet appearance. While this is a bit more work than most other recipes in the book, it's an ideal meal for occasions that warrant something special. Simply couple this entrée with a tossed green salad and bring on the guests!

SERVES 4 (SERVING SIZE: 2 CUPS)

1½ tablespoons olive oil

4 plum tomatoes, seeded and diced

12 ounces skinless halibut, cut into 1-inch pieces (or substitute striped bass or cod)

½ teaspoon kosher salt

½ teaspoon black pepper

½ medium onion, chopped

2 cloves garlic, minced

1½ cups unsalted or reduced-sodium vegetable broth

2 cups peas (fresh or frozen)

1 (12- to 14-ounce) box whole grain rotini or fusilli

1   Heat the olive oil in a large skillet over medium heat. Add the tomatoes and sauté until they begin to break down, about 4 minutes.

2   Add the halibut to the skillet and cook, occasionally stirring gently, until just opaque, about 3 minutes. Season with ¼ teaspoon of the salt and ¼ teaspoon of the black pepper. Remove the skillet from the heat; set aside.

3   Liberally coat a medium saucepan with oil spray, and preheat it over medium heat. Add the onion and garlic and sauté until softened, 3 to 5 minutes.

4   Add the vegetable broth, peas, remaining ¼ teaspoon salt, and remaining ¼ teaspoon black pepper to the pan. Bring the mixture to a boil. Then reduce the heat to low and simmer for about 5 minutes.

5   Meanwhile, bring a large pot of unsalted water to a boil.

6   Carefully transfer the peas, with all the liquid, to a blender or food processor and puree until smooth. (Alternatively, you can use an immersion blender to puree the sauce directly in the pan.) Return the puree to the pan and keep it warm over low heat, stirring occasionally.

7   Add the rotini to the boiling water and cook for 8 minutes or until al dente. Drain the pasta and gently toss it with the halibut-tomato mixture, taking care not to break up the halibut pieces.

8   To serve, ladle some of the warm pea sauce onto each serving dish, and mound some of the halibut and pasta on top of the sauce.

Nutrition Information	Calories – 524 • Protein – 36g • Carbohydrate – 80g • Total fat – 9g
	Saturated fat – 1g • Cholesterol – 25mg • Fiber – 12g • Sodium – 550mg

SPAGHETTI WITH SHRIMP AND FENNEL

This dish hits the dinner superfecta: it's delicious, nutritious, quick-cooking, and reasonably inexpensive for a seafood entrée if you buy shell-on frozen shrimp. Fennel, which looks kind of like squashed celery with wispy fronds, has a mild licorice flavor that complements shrimp and other seafood beautifully. Use your favorite jarred marinara sauce or prepare my easy homemade version. As with all my other recipes, I call for whole grain pasta, which boosts the fiber factor to keep you feeling full for hours and helps put a lid on late-night snacking. This is one of those recipes you can pull out of your hat on hectic days when putting dinner on the table seems like an impossibility.

SERVES 4 (SERVING SIZE: 2½ CUPS)

1 (12- to 14-ounce) package whole wheat spaghetti

3 cloves garlic, thinly sliced

1 bulb fennel (about 12 ounces), rough outer leaves discarded, bulb halved and thinly sliced

1 pound large shrimp, shelled and deveined (fresh or thawed from frozen)

1 teaspoon dried oregano

1½ cups marinara sauce, store-bought or homemade (page 121)

10 fresh basil leaves, torn (optional)

1   Bring a large pot of unsalted water to a boil, add the spaghetti, and cook according to the package directions.

2   While the pasta cooks, prepare the sauce: Liberally coat a large pot with oil spray, and preheat it over medium heat.

3   Add the sliced garlic and sauté until very lightly browned, 1 to 2 minutes.

4   Add the fennel and sauté for 2 to 3 minutes, or until it is just beginning to soften.

5   Raise the heat to high, add the shrimp and oregano, and sauté for 2 minutes, or until the shrimp is opaque and just cooked.

6   Add the marinara sauce and basil (if using) to the shrimp, and stir until heated through. Remove the pot from the heat.

7   Drain the pasta, and add it directly to the sauce. Toss to coat the pasta evenly with the sauce.

| Nutrition Information | Calories – 476 • Protein – 38 g • Carbohydrate – 77 g • Total fat – 4 g |
| | Saturated fat – 0.5 g • Cholesterol – 170 mg • Fiber – 3 g • Sodium – 495 mg |

POULTRY ENTRÉES

CHICKEN LETTUCE WRAPS

My kids jump at the chance to order chicken lettuce wraps from restaurant menus, so I was thrilled when I perfected this scrumptiously lighter version that I can make at home. It has all the punch of the original but with a lot fewer calories, less fat and sodium, and still a hearty dose of protein. Loaded with vegetables and chicken and spiced with ginger, garlic, cilantro, soy sauce, and rice vinegar, it's sure to please kids and adults alike. When I discovered how a manual food chopper made quick work of chopping all the veggies, I was amazed—and a true convert to this handy kitchen device. (Carefully pulsing the ingredients in a food processor works equally well.) Be sure you use soft, pliable butterhead lettuce, such as Boston or Bibb, for the lettuce cups. I promise, everyone will have fun scooping the chicken mixture into the lettuce and eating this out of hand—it makes for a perfect kid-friendly meal!

SERVES 4 (SERVING SIZE: 3 LETTUCE WRAPS)

4 medium carrots, peeled and finely diced

2 stalks celery, finely diced

1 large red bell pepper, seeded and finely diced

1 (8-ounce) can water chestnuts, drained and finely diced

3 scallions (white and green parts), thinly sliced

2 tablespoons grated or finely minced fresh ginger

4 cloves garlic, minced

1 pound ground chicken (at least 90% lean)

¼ teaspoon kosher salt

¼ teaspoon black pepper

⅓ cup bottled Chinese plum sauce

2 tablespoons reduced-sodium soy sauce

2 tablespoons rice vinegar

1 teaspoon hot chili paste, such as sriracha (or to taste)

¼ cup unsalted roasted cashews, chopped

¼ cup minced fresh cilantro, plus extra for garnish (optional)

1 head Boston or Bibb lettuce

1 Liberally coat a large skillet with oil spray, and preheat it over medium-high heat.

2   Add the carrots, celery, bell pepper, water chestnuts, scallions, ginger, and garlic. Sauté, stirring occasionally, until the vegetables soften slightly, about 5 minutes, adding a tablespoon of water at a time as necessary to prevent scorching.

3   Reapply oil spray if necessary, and add the ground chicken to the skillet. Cook until the chicken is no longer pink, breaking the meat into a fine crumble with a wooden spoon as it cooks. Season with the salt and pepper.

4   Add the plum sauce, soy sauce, vinegar, and chili paste and stir to coat. Reduce the heat to low and simmer until heated through.

5   Remove the skillet from the heat, and stir in the cashews and cilantro. Allow the mixture to cool slightly, about 5 minutes.

6   Clean the lettuce and break off 12 individual leaves (trim away the stem ends of the leaves if they are tough). Fill each lettuce cup with roughly ½ cup of the chicken mixture. Garnish with additional cilantro if desired.

Nutrition Information	Calories – 298 • Protein – 27 g • Carbohydrate – 34 g • Total fat – 9 g
	Saturated fat – 2 g • Cholesterol – 80 mg • Fiber – 5 g • Sodium – 610 mg

MEDITERRANEAN MEATLOAF

The only drawback to this mouthwatering meatloaf is portion control. You will want seconds—and maybe thirds! I call this "action packed" because there is so much going on: loads of chopped veggies, sun-dried tomatoes, Parmesan cheese, and lots of herbs to kick up the flavor. When you cut into it, it looks as though handfuls of colorful confetti had been tossed into the mixture. One caveat: making this requires a good deal of peeling and chopping. However, a food chopper will cut the prep time considerably, and in the end it's well worth the effort. I set out to make an old-style meatloaf with a few modern twists, and I believe I succeeded: this is definitely not your grandma's meatloaf.

SERVES 6

1¼ pounds lean ground turkey (at least 90% lean)

1 cup packed chopped baby spinach leaves

½ cup grated Parmesan cheese

½ cup diced roasted bell peppers

½ cup shredded zucchini (unpeeled)

¼ cup oil-packed sun-dried tomatoes, patted dry and finely diced (optional)

¼ cup finely diced celery

¼ cup grated peeled carrot

2 shallots, finely diced

1 clove garlic, minced

2 tablespoons no-salt-added tomato paste

2 teaspoons Worcestershire sauce

1 teaspoon dried oregano

½ teaspoon dried thyme

½ teaspoon kosher salt

½ teaspoon black pepper

¼ teaspoon crushed red pepper flakes

2 egg whites, beaten

1   Preheat the oven to 350°F. Line a baking sheet with aluminum foil, and coat the foil with oil spray.

2   In a large mixing bowl, combine all of the ingredients and mix until evenly distributed.

3   Transfer the mixture to the prepared baking sheet, and shape it into an elongated loaf about 2 inches thick.

4   Bake for 55 minutes, or until the internal temperature registers 160°F.

| Nutrition Information | Calories – 202 • Protein – 26 g • Carbohydrate – 8 g • Total fat – 6 g |
| | Saturated fat – 2 g • Cholesterol – 60 mg • Fiber – 1 g • Sodium – 405 mg |

CHIPOTLE CHICKEN

For a chicken dish with a serious kick, as well as incredible flavor, dive into this one. Chipotle chiles, which are smoked jalapeños, may not be the hottest chiles on the block, but they do pack a punch, so start slowly when you introduce them to your cooking. I like this super-spicy (for me, the hotter the better!), but if you're not in the same club, use just 1 chipotle the first time you make it. I make this with chicken thighs—skin removed, of course—because the dark meat stands up so well to the long, slow, fall-off-the-bone cooking. But if you prefer white meat, go ahead and use boneless, skinless breasts. Serve this as is, or over brown rice or whole wheat pasta. There's a lot of tasty sauce and you may want something to soak it all up.

SERVES 4 (SERVING SIZE: 2 CHICKEN THIGHS WITH 1 CUP SAUCE)

8 bone-in chicken thighs, skinned and trimmed of excess fat

½ teaspoon kosher salt

½ teaspoon black pepper

1⅓ cups low-fat unsalted or reduced-sodium chicken broth

6 cloves garlic, finely minced

1 medium onion, chopped into ½-inch pieces

1 red bell pepper, seeded and chopped into ½-inch pieces

1 green bell pepper, seeded and chopped into ½-inch pieces

2 tablespoons dried oregano

1 teaspoon ground cumin

Dash of cayenne pepper

1 (28-ounce) can no-salt-added crushed tomatoes

¼ cup apple cider vinegar

2 chipotle chiles in adobo sauce, chiles finely minced, 2 tablespoons adobo sauce reserved (see Note)

1   Liberally coat a large pot or Dutch oven with oil spray, and preheat it over medium-high heat.

2   Season the chicken thighs with ¼ teaspoon of the salt and ¼ teaspoon of the black pepper. Add half of the thighs to the pot and sear until golden brown on all sides, 2 to 3 minutes per side. Transfer to a plate. Brown the remaining thighs, transfer them to the plate, and set aside.

3   Add ⅓ cup of the chicken broth to the pot, being careful to avoid the steam that may rise. Use a heatproof spatula or wooden spoon to scrape up the browned bits from the bottom of the pot. Continue simmering the broth until the pan is almost dry.

4   Add the garlic, onion, and bell peppers to the pot and stir well. Cook until the vegetables have softened slightly, about 5 minutes, adding a tablespoon of water at a time as necessary to prevent scorching.

5   Add the oregano, cumin, and cayenne pepper, and cook for 1 minute.

6   Add the canned tomatoes, vinegar, chipotle chiles, adobo sauce, and remaining 1 cup chicken broth and stir well to combine. Season with the remaining ¼ teaspoon salt and ¼ teaspoon black pepper.

7   Return the chicken thighs to the pot, completely covering them with the tomato mixture, and bring the sauce to a boil. Then reduce the heat to low, cover the pot, and simmer for 20 minutes.

8   Uncover the pot and continue simmering over low heat for another 30 minutes, or until the chicken thighs are tender.

NOTE: Chipotles come packed in cans with adobo sauce, so use what you need and then freeze the extras in small plastic bags (I pack 2 or 3 per bag, with some sauce). This way, they are ready to defrost and use any time you have a yen for this dish, which in my house is pretty often!

Nutrition Information	Calories – 290 • Protein – 33 g • Carbohydrate – 20 g • Total fat – 6 g
	Saturated fat – 1 g • Cholesterol – 110 mg • Fiber – 6 g • Sodium – 440 mg

UPSIDE-DOWN PAN PIZZA
WITH THE WORKS

When you and the kids get a craving for pizza, make this instead of ordering delivery or hitting your local parlor. One serving of this fun, upside-down concoction has far less calories, fat, and sodium than a traditional New York–style slice. Between the protein-packed ground turkey, calcium-loaded cheese, and vitamin-rich veggies, this dish effortlessly delivers oodles of good nutrition. I mix onions, bell peppers, mushrooms, and tomatoes with the ground turkey, but if you like olives, hot pepper rings, spinach, broccoli, arugula—even pineapple—go for it! True to its name, the upside-down pizza gets topped with my play on pizza crust (it's actually whole wheat pancake mix); then it's sprinkled with traditional seasonings and baked in the oven. Making this dish may earn you the title of "hippest mom on the block" . . . at least for a day!

SERVES 6

1¼ pounds ground turkey or beef (at least 90% lean)

1 medium red onion, diced

1 green bell pepper, seeded and diced

2 portobello mushrooms, stems removed, caps diced

1 (28-ounce) can no-salt-added crushed tomatoes

2 teaspoons dried oregano, plus extra for sprinkling

1 teaspoon dried basil

½ teaspoon garlic powder

¼ teaspoon crushed red pepper flakes (or to taste), plus extra for sprinkling

½ teaspoon kosher salt

½ teaspoon black pepper

1½ cups (6 ounces) shredded part-skim mozzarella cheese

½ cup grated Parmesan cheese

¾ cup whole grain baking or pancake mix

1½ cups skim milk

1 large egg

2 large egg whites

1   Preheat the oven to 375°F. Coat a 13×9-inch baking dish with oil spray, and set it aside.

2   Liberally coat a large skillet with oil spray, and preheat it over medium heat.

3   Add the ground meat, onion, bell pepper, and mushrooms to the skillet and sauté until the meat is cooked through and the vegetables have softened, about 10 minutes.

4   Drain off any liquid in the skillet. Add the crushed tomatoes, oregano, basil, garlic powder, red pepper flakes, salt, and pepper, and stir to combine with the meat mixture.

5   Spoon the tomato-meat mixture into the prepared baking dish, and spread it out to form an even layer. Sprinkle evenly with the mozzarella and Parmesan cheeses.

6   In a medium bowl, whisk together the baking mix, milk, whole egg, and egg whites. Pour this batter over the cheese-topped mixture. Don't worry if the batter seems runny; it will completely cook through in the oven. Sprinkle with additional oregano and crushed red pepper to taste.

7   Bake for 30 minutes, or until the top is golden brown and a knife inserted in the center of the crust comes out clean.

8   Let cool for 5 minutes. Then cut into 6 pieces and serve.

Nutrition Information	Calories – 388 • Protein – 41 g • Carbohydrate – 27 g • Total fat – 12 g
	Saturated fat – 4 g • Cholesterol – 105 mg • Fiber – 5 g • Sodium – 690 mg

SESAME CHICKEN TENDERS

Thanks to the yummy sweet sauce, your kids will gobble up these protein-packed chicken tenders. The addictive topping is made with easy-to-find Asian ingredients—rice vinegar, soy sauce, sesame oil—that will keep for months and come in handy for other recipes. To coat the chicken I use panko bread crumbs for extra crunch. If you're lucky enough to find whole wheat panko, fantastic, but don't worry if you can only find standard white—for this recipe, it's perfectly fine. I'm pretty positive this recipe will win over your fussiest family member and soon work its way into your regular dinner rotation.

SERVES 4 (SERVING SIZE: 4 TO 5 TENDERS WITH SAUCE)

SESAME SAUCE

1 cup low-fat unsalted or reduced-sodium chicken broth

1 tablespoon grated or finely minced fresh ginger

4 cloves garlic, finely minced

2 tablespoons ketchup

2 tablespoons low-sodium soy sauce

1 tablespoon rice vinegar

1 tablespoon honey

1½ tablespoons Asian sesame oil

1½ tablespoons cornstarch

CHICKEN TENDERS

2 egg whites

1 cup panko bread crumbs

½ teaspoon kosher salt

¼ teaspoon black pepper

1½ pounds boneless, skinless chicken breasts, sliced into strips

1. Prepare the sesame sauce: In a small (1- to 2-quart) saucepan, combine the chicken broth, ginger, garlic, ketchup, soy sauce, rice vinegar, honey, and sesame oil. Bring to a simmer over medium heat.

2. In a small bowl or cup, combine the cornstarch with 3 tablespoons water. Stir together thoroughly.

3. Add the cornstarch mixture to the sauce, and stir. Simmer for 2 to 3 minutes, stirring occasionally; the mixture will develop into a thick glaze. Remove the pan from the heat and cover it to keep the sauce warm while you prepare the chicken tenders.

4   In a shallow bowl, lightly beat the egg whites until frothy.

5   In a second shallow bowl, combine the panko bread crumbs with the salt and black pepper.

6   Using tongs or your fingers, dip each chicken strip into the egg white, then lightly coat it with panko. Place the breaded chicken strip on a plate. Repeat until all the chicken strips are breaded.

7   Liberally coat a large skillet or sauté pan with oil spray, and preheat it over medium-high heat.

8   Add a batch of the chicken tenders to the skillet in a single layer, taking care not to overcrowd the pan. Cook until golden brown on the first side, 4 to 5 minutes.

9   Using tongs, flip the chicken tenders over and cook until they are browned on the second side and cooked through, 2 to 3 minutes. Transfer them to a clean plate and recoat the skillet with oil spray. Repeat until all the chicken tenders are cooked.

10 To serve, drizzle the chicken tenders with the sesame sauce, or serve the sauce on the side for dipping.

| Nutrition Information | Calories – 365 • Protein – 46 g • Carbohydrate – 26 g • Total fat – 8 g |
| | Saturated fat – 1 g • Cholesterol – 95 mg • Fiber – 2 g • Sodium – 725 mg |

CHICKEN CACCIATORE

Most cuisines have a hunter's stew—a slow-cooked pot where recently harvested vegetables meld with regional meats and favorite seasonings. This one, based on Italy's famed cacciatore, is made with chicken and tomatoes and loads of zucchini, which soaks up flavors like nothing else. I also add olives to the mix, which hold heart-healthy monounsaturated fats and add a robust layer of flavor. And as I have learned from my favorite Italian cooks, I finish the dish with a splash of good balsamic vinegar to round out the stew with its sweet, mellow acidity. The portions here are generous, and I can assure you that absolutely no one will leave the table hungry.

SERVES 4 (SERVING SIZE: 2¼ CUPS)

1½ pounds boneless, skinless chicken breasts, cut into 2-inch chunks

½ teaspoon kosher salt

½ teaspoon black pepper

3 cloves garlic, minced

1 large red onion, thinly sliced

¼ cup low-fat unsalted or reduced-sodium chicken broth (or substitute red wine)

1 (8- to 10-ounce) package cremini (baby bella) mushrooms, trimmed and quartered

2 tablespoons dried Italian herb blend (or substitute 1 tablespoon dried basil plus 1 tablespoon dried oregano)

1 (28-ounce) can no-salt-added crushed tomatoes

1 large red bell pepper, seeded and cut into 1-inch pieces

1 large yellow bell pepper, seeded and cut into 1-inch pieces

2 medium zucchini, cubed

½ cup pitted black olives, roughly chopped (optional)

2 tablespoons balsamic vinegar

1   Liberally coat a large pot or Dutch oven with oil spray, and preheat it over medium-high heat.

2   Season the chicken pieces with ¼ teaspoon of the salt and ¼ teaspoon of the black pepper. Add the chicken to the pot and cook until golden brown on all sides, 5 to 7 minutes.

3   Reapply oil spray if necessary, and then add the garlic and onion to the chicken. Sauté until the onion just begins to soften, about 3 minutes.

4   Add the chicken broth (or wine) and scrape the bottom of the pot to release any browned bits.

5   Add the mushrooms and the Italian herb blend, and cook until the mushrooms have softened, 3 to 4 minutes.

6   Add the crushed tomatoes and bell peppers, and cook for 5 minutes.

7   Add the zucchini and olives (if using), and stir well to coat all the ingredients with the tomato sauce. Season with the remaining ¼ teaspoon salt and ¼ teaspoon black pepper.

8   Reduce the heat to low, cover the pot, and simmer for 30 minutes.

9   Uncover the pot and continue to simmer for 15 minutes.

10   Stir in the balsamic vinegar just before serving.

Nutrition Information	Calories – 372 • Protein – 48 g • Carbohydrate – 31 g • Total fat – 5 g Saturated fat – 1 g • Cholesterol – 95 mg • Fiber – 8 g • Sodium – 530 mg

JOY'S TURKEY MEATBALLS
WITH EASY MARINARA SAUCE

My mom makes a mean meatball, and just the smell of them simmering away brings me back to my childhood home in Tappan, New York. My own slimmed-down version uses lean ground turkey and egg whites to keep things light, and comes loaded with the classic flavors of Parmesan cheese, onion, and garlic, plus a little minced carrot for extra sweetness and nutrition. Instead of white refined bread crumbs, I use whole grain oats as my binder. My mom taught me that the trick to super-moist meatballs is cooking them directly in the sauce, rather than baking them first. Of course, this also means less cooking time and fewer pans to clean, which makes this method a triple bonus. Toss these sensational turkey meatballs with whole wheat pasta, or serve them on whole grain buns and top them with mozzarella cheese for a quick meatball Parmesan hero. Comfort food at its best—and leanest!

SERVES 4 (SERVING SIZE: 5 MEATBALLS)

Easy Marinara Sauce (recipe follows), or 2 (26-ounce) jars store-bought marinara sauce

1 medium onion, finely chopped

1 medium carrot, peeled and finely chopped or grated

2 cloves garlic, minced, or ½ teaspoon garlic powder

¾ cup grated Parmesan cheese

1 tablespoon dried Italian herb blend (or substitute 2 teaspoons dried basil plus 2 teaspoons dried oregano)

¾ teaspoon kosher salt

¼ teaspoon black pepper

¼ teaspoon crushed red pepper flakes

1¼ pounds ground turkey (at least 90% lean)

2 large egg whites, lightly beaten

¼ cup old-fashioned or quick-cooking oats

1 Prepare the Easy Marinara Sauce or bring store-bought marinara sauce to a gentle simmer in a large pot.

2   In a large mixing bowl, stir together the onion, carrot, garlic, Parmesan cheese, Italian seasoning, salt, pepper, and red pepper flakes.

3   Add the ground turkey, egg whites, and oats. Mix thoroughly until the ingredients are well combined.

4   Shape the meat mixture into approximately 20 meatballs, 1½ inches in diameter.

5   Carefully place all the meatballs in the marinara sauce. *Do not stir;* stirring will cause the meatballs to break apart. Do not worry if some of the meatballs are not completely submerged in the sauce. Cover the pot and simmer gently for 20 minutes.

6   Remove the lid and gently stir the meatballs to thoroughly coat them with the sauce. Simmer, uncovered, for an additional 20 minutes.

Nutrition Information	Calories – 300 • Protein – 40g • Carbohydrate – 10g • Total fat – 10g
	Saturated fat – 4g • Cholesterol – 95mg • Fiber – 2g • Sodium – 720mg

EASY MARINARA SAUCE

I always keep my pantry stocked with bottled pasta sauce, but nothing beats made-from-scratch marinara (Grandma, please forgive me, I'm using canned tomatoes). This is a pretty standard recipe with an added splash of balsamic vinegar to brighten the flavor. Use it with the turkey meatballs, or pour it over grilled chicken cutlets and top it with part-skim mozzarella and grated Parmesan cheese for a light version of Chicken Parm. The sauce freezes beautifully, so consider doubling the recipe and freezing a batch for next time.

SERVES 14 (SERVING SIZE: ½ CUP)

1 large onion, finely chopped

4 cloves garlic, finely minced

2 tablespoons balsamic vinegar

2 (28-ounce) cans no-salt-added crushed tomatoes

1 tablespoon dried Italian herb blend (or substitute 2 teaspoons dried basil plus 2 teaspoons dried oregano)

½ teaspoon crushed red pepper flakes

Kosher salt and black pepper

1 Liberally coat a large pot with oil spray, and preheat it over medium heat.

2 Add the onion and cook, stirring occasionally, just until translucent, about 5 minutes.

3 Stir in the garlic and balsamic vinegar and cook for 1 minute.

4 Add the tomatoes, Italian seasoning, and red pepper flakes, and bring to a boil. Then reduce the heat to low and simmer gently for 30 minutes. Season with salt and black pepper to taste.

Nutrition Information	Calories – 51 • Protein – 2g • Carbohydrate – 9g • Total fat – 0g
	Saturated fat – 0g • Cholesterol – 0mg • Fiber – 2g • Sodium – 20mg

BRAISED TURKEY SAUSAGE AND CABBAGE

In the spirit of Oktoberfest, I've created a hearty one-pot supper that brings together three German favorites: sausage, cabbage, and beer. I use lean poultry sausage, which has all the spicy, meaty goodness of beef or pork sausage with minimal saturated fat. Sweet caramelized onions lay the foundation for the dish, and the cabbage, which I slice into long, thin strips, has a texture vaguely reminiscent of pasta—but with a fraction of the calories. Beer serves as my braising liquid (choose a dark, robust brew to emphasize the stew's earthy flavor) and drives home the dish's German heritage. For this one, make sure you come to the table with an appetite.

SERVES 6 (SERVING SIZE: 2½ CUPS)

6 links Italian turkey dinner sausages

1 large onion, thinly sliced

1 tablespoon granulated sugar

1 medium head green cabbage, thinly sliced or shredded

1 (12-ounce) bottle beer, preferably a dark beer although any variety will work (or substitute 1½ cups low-fat unsalted or reduced-sodium chicken broth)

3 tablespoons apple cider vinegar

2 tablespoons spicy brown mustard

1 bay leaf

½ teaspoon kosher salt

¼ teaspoon black pepper

1   Liberally coat a large pot with oil spray, and preheat it over medium heat.

2   Add the sausages and cook, turning them as needed, until browned on all sides, about 8 minutes (the sausages will still be raw in the center). Transfer the sausages to a plate.

3   Return the pot to medium heat and reapply oil spray, liberally coating the bottom of the pot.

4   Add the onion and sugar, and cook, stirring often, until the onion is caramelized (golden brown in color), 10 to 12 minutes. As the onion cooks, add a tablespoon of water at a time, as necessary, to help soften the onion and scrape up any browned bits that have formed on the bottom of the pan.

5   While the onions caramelize, slice the partially cooked sausages into ¼-inch-thick rounds. Set aside.

6   Add the cabbage, beer (or broth), vinegar, mustard, bay leaf, salt, and pepper to the caramelized onion. Raise the heat to medium-high and bring the liquid to a boil, stirring and working the cabbage down into the pot as it begins to wilt.

7   Add the sliced sausages and toss with the cabbage mixture until well combined. Reduce the heat to low, cover, and simmer, stirring occasionally to ensure that all the ingredients are evenly mixed, for 25 to 30 minutes, or until the cabbage is tender. Discard the bay leaf before serving.

Nutrition Information	Calories – 232 • Protein – 20g • Carbohydrate – 18g • Total fat – 9g
	Saturated fat – 3g • Cholesterol – 50mg • Fiber – 4g • Sodium – 800mg

CHICKEN CORDON BLEU

If you are among those who absolutely love this classic French dish—chicken stuffed with Gruyère cheese and ham and then fried (yikes!)—you are in luck. I have figured out how to slash the calories and fat and still keep the rich, opulent flavors alive. I fill the chicken breasts with reduced-fat Swiss cheese and super-lean Canadian bacon, and instead of frying, I simmer them in broth. Mushrooms and rosemary add a unique earthy finish to the filling. Believe me, there is no sacrifice in taste, and for about 250 calories a serving, you can indulge in the rich flavors without one stitch of guilt.

SERVES 4 (SERVING SIZE: 1 STUFFED CHICKEN ROLL WITH SAUCE)

1 large shallot, finely chopped

4 large cremini (baby bella) mushrooms, trimmed and diced

2 slices Canadian bacon, diced

1 teaspoon crushed dried rosemary, or 2 teaspoons minced fresh rosemary

2 large skinless, boneless chicken breasts (at least 8 ounces each; see Note)

¼ teaspoon black pepper

4 slices reduced-fat Swiss cheese, chopped

1 cup low-fat unsalted or reduced-sodium chicken broth

1   Liberally coat a large skillet with oil spray; preheat it over medium-high heat.

2   Add the shallot and cook until softened, about 3 minutes.

3   Add the mushrooms and cook until softened, 2 to 3 minutes.

4   Add the Canadian bacon and rosemary, and cook for 3 to 4 minutes. Transfer the mushroom mixture to a bowl to cool. Reserve the skillet.

5   Prepare the chicken breasts: Holding your knife parallel to the cutting board, carefully slice each breast in half horizontally to form 2 thin cutlets. Place each chicken cutlet on a sheet of plastic wrap and cover it with a second sheet of wrap. Pound each piece with a flat meat mallet, rolling pin, or heavy can to a thickness of ¼ inch. Season the chicken cutlets on one side with the black pepper.

6   Mix half of the chopped Swiss cheese into the cooled mushroom-bacon mixture, reserving the other half of the cheese in the refrigerator.

7   Spoon 2 to 3 tablespoons of the mushroom-bacon-cheese mixture down the center of the seasoned side of each chicken cutlet. Starting at the narrower end, roll the chicken into a log to fully enclose the filling. Secure with toothpicks.

8   Preheat the skillet over medium heat. Liberally coat it with oil spray.

9   Place the chicken rolls in the skillet, seam side down. Cook, turning the rolls as needed, to a golden brown on all sides, 2 to 3 minutes per side.

10 Add the chicken broth to the skillet, cover, and cook over medium heat for 10 to 12 minutes, or until the chicken is cooked through, turning the rolls once halfway through.

11 When the chicken is fully cooked, remove the rolls from the broth, place them on a serving platter, and cover with aluminum foil to keep warm (remove the toothpicks when cool enough to touch).

12 Return the skillet to the stove, raise the heat to medium-high, and bring the broth to a boil. Reduce the broth to about ½ cup to form a sauce, scraping the bottom of the pan to release any browned bits.

13 To serve, pour the sauce over the chicken rolls and sprinkle with the remaining chopped Swiss cheese.

NOTE: You can use 4 thin chicken cutlets if you'd like to skip the step of slicing and pounding the chicken breasts. Be sure to select cutlets with a large surface area in order to accommodate the filling.

Nutrition Information	Calories – 252 • Protein – 44 g • Carbohydrate – 4 g • Total fat – 7 g
	Saturated fat – 3 g • Cholesterol – 95 mg • Fiber – 0 g • Sodium – 305 mg

TURKEY THYME MEATBALLS
WITH LEMONY CREAM SAUCE

This French-inspired entrée will please sophisticated palates with its rich, thyme-kissed flavor and piquant, creamy yogurt sauce. The meatballs are incredibly moist and tender and the sauce, spiked with lemon zest, adds a subtle zing to the dish. I serve this with green beans and carrots, which draw out the delicate flavors of the cream sauce and of course add an enormous amount of nutrition. This dish elevates the familiar meatball from standard kid-friendly fare to downright gourmet goodness.

SERVES 4 (SERVING SIZE: 1¾ CUPS, ABOUT 8 MEATBALLS WITH SAUCE)

1¼ pounds ground turkey (at least 90% lean)

¼ cup unseasoned whole wheat bread crumbs

1 large egg, beaten

½ teaspoon dried thyme

½ teaspoon garlic powder

1½ teaspoons Worcestershire sauce

¾ cup nonfat plain yogurt

¾ teaspoon kosher salt

½ teaspoon black pepper

2 cups low-fat unsalted or reduced-sodium chicken broth

2 cups green beans, trimmed and halved crosswise

2 cups shredded peeled carrots (about 4 medium carrots)

1½ tablespoons cornstarch

Grated zest of 1 large lemon

1   In a large bowl, combine the ground turkey, bread crumbs, egg, thyme, garlic powder, Worcestershire sauce, ¼ cup of the yogurt, ¼ teaspoon of the salt, and ¼ teaspoon of the black pepper, taking care not to overwork the mixture.

2   Form heaping teaspoonfuls of the meat mixture into small meatballs. The mixture should make 30 to 35 meatballs.

3   In a large pot (wide enough to fit all the meatballs in a single layer), bring 1¾ cups of the chicken broth to a boil over medium-high heat.

4   Add the meatballs in a single layer and return the broth to a boil. Reduce the heat to low, cover the pot, and simmer until the meatballs are cooked through, about 10 minutes. Using a slotted spoon, carefully transfer the meatballs to a clean bowl, and cover to keep warm.

5   Add the green beans and carrots to the broth and bring to a boil over medium-high heat. Cover, and cook until the vegetables are crisp-tender, about 3 minutes.

6   While the vegetables cook, in a medium bowl, whisk together the remaining ¼ cup broth, remaining ½ cup yogurt, cornstarch, lemon zest, and the remaining ½ teaspoon salt and ¼ teaspoon black pepper.

7   Stir the yogurt mixture into the vegetable-broth mixture in the pot, and bring to a boil. Continue stirring until the mixture has thickened, about 1 minute.

8   Return the meatballs to the pot and stir gently to coat them evenly with the sauce. Cook for 2 minutes or until the meatballs are warmed through.

Nutrition Information	Calories – 319 • Protein – 39 g • Carbohydrate – 23 g • Total fat – 7 g
	Saturated fat – 2 g • Cholesterol – 135 mg • Fiber – 4 g • Sodium – 720 mg

CRISPY PARMESAN CHICKEN

These baked chicken breasts are so crispy and crunchy, you'd swear they came straight from the deep fryer! It's obvious that oven-baked chicken cutlets are much more figure-friendly than the type fried in a vat of oil, but they have a tendency to come out soggy or chewy. I get around that problem by using a Parmesan cheese coating that browns up beautifully in a hot oven. For a dose of added nutrition and extra crunch, I mix in ground flaxseed with the cheese. Here, I use standard chicken breasts and butterfly them open like a book to make them thinner—and ultimately crispier—but you can skip this step and use thin chicken cutlets. I think these cutlets are plenty flavorful on their own, but feel free to dunk them in ketchup, barbecue sauce, or marinara sauce for a little extra fun.

SERVES 4 (SERVING SIZE: 1 LARGE CHICKEN BREAST)

4 boneless, skinless chicken breasts (about 1½ pounds, see Note)

¼ cup nonfat or low-fat buttermilk (shake well before measuring)

½ cup whole wheat flour (or substitute any other type of flour)

1 teaspoon onion powder

½ teaspoon kosher salt

½ teaspoon black pepper

3 egg whites

1 tablespoon skim milk (or substitute water)

2 teaspoons hot sauce

¾ cup finely grated Parmesan cheese

¼ cup ground flaxseed

1   Butterfly the chicken breasts: Holding your knife parallel to the cutting board, carefully slice into each breast horizontally, taking care not to slice all the way through the meat. Fold each chicken breast open like a book so it lies flat.

2   Place the chicken breasts in a resealable plastic bag. Add the buttermilk to the bag and seal it. Squish the contents around to ensure all of the chicken is coated with buttermilk. Marinate for at least 30 minutes, or up to 24 hours.

3   Preheat the oven to 425°F. Line a baking sheet with aluminum foil, and coat the foil with oil spray.

4   Set out 3 shallow dishes for a three-step breading station.

5   In the first dish, combine the flour, onion powder, salt, and black pepper; mix well.

6   In the second dish, combine the egg whites, milk, and hot sauce; whisk together until slightly frothy.

7   In the third dish, combine the Parmesan cheese and flaxseed; mix well.

8   Shake the excess buttermilk off one of the chicken breasts, and press it into the first dish (with seasoned flour), coating both sides. Shake off the excess flour, and then dip it into the second dish (with the egg white mixture), coating both sides. Finally, lay the chicken in the third dish, coating both sides with the cheese-flaxseed mixture. Place the coated chicken breast on the prepared baking sheet, and repeat with the remaining 3 chicken breasts.

9   Mist the top of each breaded chicken breast with oil spray.

10   Bake for 25 to 35 minutes, or until browned and crispy.

NOTE: Alternatively, use 1½ pounds thin chicken cutlets, and skip step 1 of the directions.

Nutrition Information	Calories – 350 • Protein – 51g • Carbohydrate – 13g • Total fat – 10g
	Saturated fat – 3g • Cholesterol – 110mg • Fiber – 3g • Sodium – 700mg

LEMON-SAGE CHICKEN BREASTS

Few things are as homey and satisfying as perfectly moist roast chicken. Most of the chicken recipes in this cookbook call for boneless, skinless breasts, which I love for their convenience, but when I'm roasting chicken in the oven I prefer to use the bone-in variety. The bones add a lot of flavor and moisture, and if you remove the skin, the calories and fat are exactly the same as for boneless breasts. The lemon and sage perfume the chicken as it cooks and make for a beautiful presentation straight from the oven. Every home cook needs a simple, succulent roast chicken recipe up his or her sleeve. This one is mine, and I'm delighted to share it with you.

SERVES 4 (SERVING SIZE: 1 CHICKEN BREAST)

4 bone-in chicken breasts, skin and excess fat removed

½ teaspoon kosher salt

¼ teaspoon black pepper

1 teaspoon dried thyme

16 fresh sage leaves

1 to 2 lemons, thinly sliced

1 Preheat the oven to 400°F. Line a baking sheet with aluminum foil, and coat the foil with oil spray.

2 Place the chicken breasts on the prepared baking sheet, bone side down.

3 Sprinkle the salt, black pepper, and thyme over the chicken. Place 4 fresh sage leaves on top of each breast, and then top the sage leaves with lemon slices (2 to 3 slices per chicken breast, depending on its size).

4 Roast on the middle oven rack for 40 to 50 minutes, until the inside is no longer pink when slit with a knife or the internal temperature reads 160°F.

Nutrition Information	Calories – 262 • Protein – 55 g • Carbohydrate – 1 g • Total fat – 3 g
	Saturated fat – 1 g • Cholesterol – 135 mg • Fiber – 0 g • Sodium – 390 mg

BEEF & PORK ENTRÉES

BEEF AND BELL PEPPER STIR-FRY

If you were raised eating beef, there are times when nothing else will satisfy—not chicken, fish, eggs, and certainly not tofu. When Ian or the kids get this craving, I often turn to a stir-fry. Flank steak, a fairly lean cut of meat with lots of good beefy flavor, takes beautifully to marinating. I load up the wok with lots of different vegetables, which is a good way to stretch the meat and bump up the nutrition. What you get is a heaping, healthful portion for only 325 calories, while the same amount of take-out stir-fry from your local Chinese restaurant can easily top 1,000 calories! Feel free to substitute chicken or shrimp for the beef, and swap any of the veggies for others you have on hand, such as eggplant, sugar snap peas, baby corn, snow peas, or mushrooms. Serve this as is or over steamed brown rice to sop up all the delicious sauce.

SERVES 4 (SERVING SIZE: 2½ CUPS)

MARINADE

¼ cup reduced-sodium soy sauce

4 teaspoons Chinese rice wine, mirin, or dry sherry

1½ teaspoons Asian sesame oil

1½ teaspoons canola oil

1 teaspoon granulated sugar

½ teaspoon black pepper

STIR-FRY

1 pound flank steak, cut into ¼-inch-thick slices against the grain

2 cups broccoli florets

2 cups green beans, trimmed and cut into 1-inch pieces

3 cloves garlic, minced

1 tablespoon grated or finely minced fresh ginger

1 medium onion, thinly sliced

1 yellow bell pepper, seeded and thinly sliced

1 red bell pepper, seeded and thinly sliced

2 teaspoons cornstarch

3 scallions (white and green parts), thinly sliced on an angle (optional)

1   Combine all the marinade ingredients in a large bowl, and stir in 2 tablespoons water.

2   Add the sliced steak to the marinade and stir to coat. Cover the bowl with plastic wrap and allow the meat to marinate in the refrigerator for a minimum of 15 minutes or up to 4 hours.

3   While the meat marinates, place the broccoli florets and cut green beans in a microwave-safe bowl, and sprinkle with about 2 tablespoons water. Microwave on high power for 2 minutes. Drain, and set aside.

4   Liberally coat a large skillet or wok with oil spray, and preheat it over medium-high heat.

5   Add the garlic and ginger and stir-fry until the garlic is lightly golden, about 30 seconds. Do not allow the garlic or ginger to burn.

6   Add the steak to the skillet, reserving the marinade in the bowl. Stir the steak continuously until it is cooked through, about 3 minutes. Transfer the steak and any juices to a clean plate.

7   Return the skillet to medium-high heat and liberally reapply oil spray.

8   Add the onions and bell peppers to the skillet. Sauté until the vegetables begin to soften, 2 to 4 minutes.

9   Add the broccoli and green beans, and continue stir-frying for about 2 minutes.

10   Stir the cornstarch into the reserved steak marinade.

11   Push the vegetables to the outskirts of the skillet, forming a well in the center. Add the marinade to the well and bring it to a boil. Then toss it thoroughly with the vegetables to coat them evenly.

12   Return the steak to the skillet and stir to combine.

13   Transfer the stir-fry to a serving dish, and garnish with the scallions if desired.

Nutrition Information	Calories – 327 • Protein – 29 g • Carbohydrate – 26 g • Total fat – 12 g
	Saturated fat – 4 g • Cholesterol – 45 mg • Fiber – 5 g • Sodium – 560 mg

SPICE-RUBBED FLANK STEAK
WITH CHIMICHURRI

Flank steak has great flavor and texture when cooked right and then properly cut—which means sliced across the grain into thin strips. It also takes really well to rubs and marinades. Here, I go the dry rub route and season the meat with my signature blend of herbs and spices. Be sure to give the rub plenty of time to sink into the meat; the longer you leave it, the better. Chimichurri is a vibrant green condiment with roots in Argentina, full of concentrated flavor and typically made with lots of olive oil. I use far less oil—no surprise there—and add a little Dijon mustard and shallot to kick up the flavor. The chimichurri is potent, so it takes only a touch to make a delicious impression.

SERVES 4 (SERVING SIZE: 4 OUNCES STEAK WITH 2 TABLESPOONS CHIMICHURRI)

SPICE RUB

1 tablespoon chili powder

2 teaspoons dried oregano

1 teaspoon garlic powder

1 teaspoon onion powder

½ teaspoon ground coriander

½ teaspoon ground cumin

½ teaspoon kosher salt

¼ teaspoon black pepper

⅛ teaspoon cayenne pepper

STEAK

1 flank steak (1 to 1½ pounds)

CHIMICHURRI

1 tablespoon olive oil

2 teaspoons Dijon mustard

Juice of 1 lemon

¼ teaspoon kosher salt

¼ teaspoon black pepper

1 clove garlic, coarsely chopped

1 shallot, coarsely chopped

½ cup packed Italian (flat-leaf) parsley leaves

2 teaspoons dried oregano

1   Prepare the spice rub: Combine all the spice rub ingredients in a small bowl and mix well.

2   Rub the spice mixture over the entire surface of the flank steak. Cover the steak with plastic wrap and store in the refrigerator for at least 30 minutes or as long as overnight.

3   Prepare the chimichurri: In a blender or food processor, combine the olive oil, Dijon mustard, lemon juice, salt, pepper, and 1 tablespoon water, and blend well. Add the garlic and shallot, and pulse to chop them fine. Add the parsley and oregano, and pulse several times to combine. Refrigerate until ready to use.

4   Preheat the broiler. Line a broiler pan or heavy baking sheet with aluminum foil, and coat the foil with oil spray.

5   Unwrap the steak and place it on the prepared baking sheet. Broil for 6 minutes on the first side.

6   Flip the steak over and broil for 4 to 5 minutes on the second side for medium doneness.

7   Remove the steak from the broiler and let it rest for 10 minutes before slicing.

8   To serve, slice the flank steak across the grain into thin slices. Top the slices with the chimichurri.

Nutrition Information	Calories – 265 • Protein – 32 g • Carbohydrate – 5 g • Total fat – 13 g
	Saturated fat – 4 g • Cholesterol – 55 mg • Fiber – 1 g • Sodium – 510 mg

BEEF TENDERLOIN
WITH FIG REDUCTION

While it's true that beef tenderloin can be pricy, it's also incredibly lean and well worth the splurge on special occasions. Because the steaks are a bit of an investment, you'll want to cook them with care. I suggest using the restaurant method of searing the meat on the stovetop and then transferring it to the oven to finish cooking. And although the meat is delicious (and offers up iron-rich protein), it's the sauce that *really* makes this dish. It's made from dried figs, which are loaded with fiber and potassium. The figs, together with the wine, garlic, and shallots, make this reduction taste like a sauce from the finest of restaurants.

SERVES 4 (SERVING SIZE: 1 MEDALLION WITH SAUCE)

1 large shallot, minced

1 clove garlic, minced

1½ cups dry red wine

6 dried figs, sliced

½ teaspoon dried thyme

½ teaspoon black pepper

1½ cups low-fat unsalted or reduced-sodium beef broth

4 (4-ounce) beef tenderloin medallions

¼ teaspoon kosher salt

1   Preheat the oven to 400°F.

2   Liberally coat a large saucepan with oil spray, and preheat it over medium heat.

3   Add the shallot and garlic and sauté until golden, 2 to 3 minutes.

4   Raise the heat to medium-high and add the wine, figs, thyme, and ¼ teaspoon of the black pepper. Bring the sauce to a rolling boil and cook until the liquid has reduced by about 90%, 8 to 10 minutes.

5   Add the beef broth and return the sauce to a boil. Continue cooking until the sauce has reduced to 1 cup, about 10 minutes.

6   While the sauce reduces, prepare the steaks: Liberally coat a large ovenproof skillet or sauté pan with oil spray, and preheat it over medium-high heat (see Note).

7   Season the tenderloin medallions with the salt and the remaining ¼ teaspoon black pepper.

8   Place the medallions in the hot skillet. Sear on the first side, 2 to 3 minutes.

9   Flip the medallions over and immediately transfer the pan to the oven. Cook for about 7 minutes for medium doneness.

10   To serve, top each medallion with about ¼ cup of the fig reduction.

NOTE: If you don't have an ovenproof skillet, sear the meat for 2 to 3 minutes on each side and then transfer the medallions to a shallow roasting pan before placing them in the oven.

Nutrition Information	Calories – 274 • Protein – 27 g • Carbohydrate – 12 g • Total fat – 6 g
	Saturated fat – 3 g • Cholesterol – 60 mg • Fiber – 1 g • Sodium – 235 mg

SPICY PORK TACOS
WITH SASSY SLAW

You'll fall in love with these colorful tacos. I make them with pork tenderloin, the leanest cut of pork and one of the easiest to cook. The meat is simmered with a lot of seasonings, some of them spicy to kick up the heat. Once the pork is cooked to perfection, it's shredded and loaded into corn tortillas. Then I top it with a super-easy coleslaw dressed with nothing but vinegar, lime juice, and a hint of honey to cut the deep spiciness of the pork and add a delightful crunch. This slaw is also great alongside other grilled or summertime foods, and of course it's made with cabbage, one of my favorite cruciferous vegetables, known for its cancer-fighting properties. The dish's bright colors and sassy personality make it festive and fun—the perfect pick for your next summer gathering.

SERVES 6 (SERVING SIZE: 2 TACOS WITH TOPPINGS AND SLAW)

PORK FILLING

1 pork tenderloin (1 to 1½ pounds), trimmed of fat

¾ teaspoon kosher salt

¼ teaspoon black pepper

4 cups low-fat unsalted or reduced-sodium chicken broth

10 black peppercorns

2 bay leaves

1 medium onion, thinly sliced

1 red bell pepper, seeded and thinly sliced

3 cloves garlic, minced

1 teaspoon ground cumin

2 teaspoons dried oregano

2 teaspoons chili powder

1 (15-ounce) can no-salt-added diced tomatoes

1 (4-ounce) can diced green chiles (with liquid)

SASSY SLAW

1 (14- to 16-ounce) bag coleslaw mix

2 large carrots, peeled

¼ cup apple cider vinegar

Juice of 1 large lime

¼ teaspoon crushed red pepper flakes

4 teaspoons honey

½ teaspoon kosher salt

TORTILLAS AND GARNISHES

12 corn tortillas

¾ cup nonfat sour cream

Chopped fresh cilantro (optional)

Lime wedges (optional)

1   Pat the pork tenderloin dry with paper towels. Sprinkle the meat on all sides with ¼ teaspoon of the salt and the black pepper.

2   Liberally coat a large pot with oil spray, and preheat it over medium-high heat.

3   Place the tenderloin in the pot and cook until browned on all sides, 2 to 3 minutes per side.

4   Pour the chicken broth into the pot and add enough water to just cover the tenderloin.

5   Add the peppercorns and bay leaves, and bring the liquid to a boil. Reduce the heat to low, partially cover the pot, and simmer the tenderloin until cooked through, about 40 minutes.

6   Remove the tenderloin from the pot and set it aside to cool. Discard the cooking liquid and solids that form in the pot (you will reuse this pot to make the pork filling).

7   While the meat is cooling, prepare the Sassy Slaw: Place the coleslaw mix in a large mixing bowl. Cut the carrots into long thin ribbons with a vegetable peeler, or grate them on the large side of a box grater. Add the carrots to the coleslaw mix and toss to combine.

8   In a small bowl, prepare the coleslaw dressing: Whisk together the cider vinegar, lime juice, red pepper flakes, honey, and salt. Pour the dressing over the coleslaw mixture and toss well. Store in the refrigerator.

9   When the tenderloin is cool enough to handle, shred the meat into thin strips, and reserve.

10 Return the pot to medium heat and liberally coat it with oil spray.

11   Add the onion, red bell pepper, garlic, cumin, oregano, and chili powder, and cook until the onion is soft, about 5 minutes.

12   Add the shredded pork, tomatoes, and green chiles, and simmer until heated through, about 10 minutes.

13   While the pork filling is simmering, preheat the oven to 350°F. Arrange the corn tortillas on a baking sheet, overlapping them as necessary, and bake uncovered for 8 to 10 minutes to warm them.

14   Meanwhile, remove the pork filling from the heat, and cover the pot to keep it warm.

15   To serve, fill each tortilla with about ½ cup of the pork mixture, and garnish with 1 tablespoon of the sour cream. Add the cilantro and lime wedges if desired. Top each taco with about ⅔ cup of the Sassy Slaw, or serve it alongside.

Nutrition Information	Calories – 327 • Protein – 27 g • Carbohydrate – 46 g • Total fat – 4 g
	Saturated fat – 1 g • Cholesterol – 60 mg • Fiber – 9 g • Sodium – 755 mg

HERB-ROASTED PORK TENDERLOIN

When it comes to pork, the tenderloin is by far your best bet—it's affordable, tender, and incredibly lean. In fact, there's only 1 gram of saturated fat in each serving of this roast, which, quite frankly, is phenomenal for a meat entrée. I rub the pork with a paste made of olive oil, lemon zest, and a fabulous herb mixture called *herbes de Provence*, easily found in the spice section of your supermarket. Although the herbs in this blend vary from brand to brand, they are meant to conjure up the sunny flavors of the South of France and nearly always include thyme, savory, and fennel seeds. In order to brown the crust and keep the meat moist, I sear the pork tenderloin on top of the stove before roasting it in the oven. If you're looking for the perfect side dish to pair with this entrée, check out the Balsamic-Glazed Pearl Onions on page 183 or the Roasted Squash with Pine Nuts on page 182.

SERVES 4

1 pork tenderloin (1 to 1½ pounds), trimmed of fat

¼ teaspoon kosher salt

¼ teaspoon black pepper

2 teaspoons dry mustard

2 teaspoons herbes de Provence seasoning blend (see Note)

1 teaspoon grated lemon zest

2 teaspoons olive oil

1   Preheat the oven to 400°F. Line a baking sheet with aluminum foil, and coat the foil with oil spray.

2   Liberally coat a large skillet with oil spray, and preheat it over medium heat.

3   Season the pork tenderloin on all sides with the salt and pepper.

4   Place the tenderloin in the hot skillet and cook until browned on all sides, 2 to 3 minutes per side.

5   Transfer the tenderloin to the prepared baking sheet.

6   In a small bowl, combine the dry mustard, herbes de Provence, lemon zest, and olive oil to form a thick paste. Rub the paste on all sides of the pork tenderloin.

7   Place the tenderloin in the oven and roast for 25 to 30 minutes, until the internal temperature of the pork reaches 160°F.

8   Remove the roast from the oven and allow it to rest for 10 minutes before slicing.

NOTE: For a different flavor, substitute dried Italian herb blend for the herbes de Provence.

Nutrition Information	Calories – 175 • Protein – 30g • Carbohydrate – 0g • Total fat – 5g Saturated fat – 1g • Cholesterol – 90mg • Fiber – 0g • Sodium – 195mg

FISH & SEAFOOD ENTRÉES

HOISIN-GLAZED SALMON

Salmon is one of the true superstars in the world of nutrition. It's a valuable source of omega-3 fatty acids, which enhance heart health, improve memory, reduce inflammation, and promote healthy joints, skin, and mood. It is also rich in vitamin D, a critical nutrient that optimizes bone health. But what really gets me going is how unbelievably fabulous this salmon dish *tastes*. The glaze is thick, shiny, and deliciously sweet—the perfect vehicle to get your "I don't eat fish"-kids to finally eat fish. I make the glaze with hoisin sauce (available at most major supermarkets), which is a rich, fragrant paste with the distinctive notes of spicy, sweet, and salt so beloved in classic Chinese cuisine.

SERVES 4 (SERVING SIZE: 1 GLAZED SALMON FILLET)

3 tablespoons hoisin sauce

3 tablespoons pure maple syrup

1 tablespoon white wine vinegar or rice vinegar

1 teaspoon grated or finely minced fresh ginger

4 (6-ounce) salmon fillets (about 1 inch thick)

1   Preheat the oven to 400°F. Line a baking sheet with aluminum foil, and coat the foil with oil spray.

2   In a small bowl, mix together the hoisin sauce, maple syrup, vinegar, and ginger to form a thick glaze.

3   Place the salmon fillets on the prepared baking sheet, spacing them evenly. Bake for 10 minutes.

4   Remove the baking sheet from the oven and smear the hoisin glaze evenly over the fillets. Return the salmon to the oven and bake until the fillets are just opaque in the center, about 5 minutes. Transfer to a platter; serve immediately.

Nutrition Information	Calories – 300 • Protein – 34g • Carbohydrate – 14g • Total fat – 11g
	Saturated fat – 2g • Cholesterol – 90mg • Fiber – 0g • Sodium – 235mg

SHRIMP SCAMPI
WITH BROCCOLI RABE AND RED PEPPER

Because shrimp scampi is one of the most popular (and caloric) seafood entrées on restaurant menus, I was eager to perfect a guilt-free version that I could regularly make at home. This recipe uses a light combination of olive oil and soft-tub margarine spread to give the scampi its characteristic buttery taste—and white wine, lemon, and plenty of garlic add to its authenticity. While the red bell pepper and broccoli rabe are certainly not traditional, they pump up the volume and nutrition by leaps and bounds. One serving provides a hearty dose of fiber, vitamin C, vitamin K, folate, and potassium. With all these extra veggies, you can absolutely enjoy this as a stand-alone dinner—but if you're yearning for pasta, feel free to serve the scampi over whole grain spaghetti or linguine. *Bon appétit!*

SERVES 4 (SERVING SIZE: 2 CUPS)

1 (16-ounce) bunch broccoli rabe, trimmed and cut into 1-inch pieces

2 tablespoons trans-fat-free reduced-fat soft tub margarine spread

1 tablespoon olive oil

2 cloves garlic, minced

¼ cup minced onion

¼ teaspoon crushed red pepper flakes (or to taste)

1 large red bell pepper, seeded and cut into 1-inch pieces

1½ pounds large shrimp, peeled and deveined

½ teaspoon kosher salt

¼ teaspoon black pepper

¼ cup dry white wine

Juice of 1 lemon

1   Blanche the broccoli rabe: Bring a large pot of unsalted water to a boil, and add the broccoli rabe. Return to a boil, and cook for 1 minute. Drain the broccoli rabe, let it cool slightly, and then squeeze the moisture out; set it aside.

2   In a large sauté pan or skillet, heat the margarine and olive oil over medium-high heat.

3   Add the garlic, onion, and red pepper flakes and sauté for 1 minute.

4   Add the red bell pepper and sauté for 2 minutes, or until the pepper is crisp-tender.

5   Add the shrimp and sauté over high heat until they are just opaque and cooked through, 3 to 4 minutes. Season with the salt and black pepper.

6   Add the wine and simmer until it has reduced by about half.

7   Add the reserved broccoli rabe and the lemon juice, and toss with the shrimp mixture until just heated through. Remove from the heat, and serve.

Nutrition Information	Calories – 293 • Protein – 39g • Carbohydrate – 10g • Total fat – 10g
	Saturated fat – 2g • Cholesterol – 255mg • Fiber – 4g • Sodium – 560mg

SPICY SHRIMP JAMBALAYA

When my husband, Ian, first tasted this jambalaya, he couldn't believe it was actually good for him. While this dish has all the elements of the much beloved Cajun stew, it clearly does not have the exorbitant calories or artery-clogging fat. I use Canadian bacon in place of sausage for good meaty flavor, and heaps of naturally low-cal shrimp to bulk up the protein. Then I load the jambalaya with lots of nutrient-dense vegetables and wholesome brown rice and season it with a generous hit of herbs and spices. Ian requests this jambalaya whenever we have large family gatherings and I am always happy to oblige. We love it spicy hot (bring on the cayenne!), but when serving to guests, know your audience and adjust the heat accordingly. This version is medium spicy.

SERVES 4 (SERVING SIZE: 2½ CUPS)

4 cloves garlic, finely minced

1 medium onion, diced

1 large green bell pepper, seeded and diced

5 stalks celery, diced

6 slices Canadian bacon, diced

1 (28-ounce) can no-salt-added diced tomatoes

¼ teaspoon cayenne pepper

1 tablespoon paprika

1 tablespoon dried marjoram

1 tablespoon dried oregano

1 tablespoon dried thyme

2 teaspoons hot sauce

1 cup long-grain brown rice

3 cups low-fat unsalted or reduced-sodium chicken broth

1 pound shrimp, peeled and deveined

1 Liberally coat a large pot or Dutch oven with oil spray, and preheat it over medium-high heat.

2 Add the garlic, onion, bell pepper, and celery and cook until the vegetables are beginning to soften, about 5 minutes, adding a tablespoon of water at a time as necessary to prevent scorching.

3   Reduce the heat to medium and add the Canadian bacon, tomatoes, spices, herbs, and hot sauce, stirring well to combine. Cook for 5 minutes.

4   Add the brown rice and chicken broth, stir well, and bring to a boil.

5   Reduce the heat to low, cover the pot, and cook for 45 minutes or until the rice is fully cooked. (Check the pot after 35 to 40 minutes, and if the dish is too dry or the rice is underdone, add extra water or broth in ¼-cup increments.)

6   Add the shrimp, cover the pot, and cook until the shrimp are pink and opaque, about 5 minutes.

Nutrition Information	Calories – 444 • Protein – 40 g • Carbohydrate – 57 g • Total fat – 6 g
	Saturated fat – 2 g • Cholesterol – 190 mg • Fiber – 8 g • Sodium – 850 mg

FISH TACOS
WITH BUTTERMILK-PARSLEY DRESSING

Fish tacos seem to be all the rage these days. While most use fried fish, I sauté mild-flavored tilapia for a light, healthful dish. If you prefer another fish, substitute halibut, mahi-mahi, or catfish. The buttermilk dressing cools the tacos and balances out the smokiness of the ancho chile powder. (FYI: Despite its name and creamy richness, buttermilk is surprisingly low in calories and fat.) The parsley in the sauce adds a vibrant pop of green, and the lemon juice brightens everything as only citrus can. Go ahead, liven up your dinner table and bring a taste of Southern California to your doorstep with these zesty wrap-ups.

SERVES 4 (SERVING SIZE: 2 TACOS WITH TOPPINGS)

BUTTERMILK-PARSLEY DRESSING

¼ cup nonfat sour cream

¼ cup nonfat or low-fat buttermilk (shake well before measuring)

2 tablespoons chopped fresh parsley

1 clove garlic, finely minced

½ teaspoon black pepper

¼ teaspoon kosher salt

TACOS

8 (6-inch) corn tortillas

4 (6-ounce) tilapia fillets

1 tablespoon ancho chile powder

¼ teaspoon kosher salt

4 cups mixed greens or shredded lettuce

1 cup cherry or grape tomatoes, halved lengthwise

1 lemon, cut into wedges

1 Preheat the oven to 350°F.

2 Prepare the buttermilk dressing: In a medium bowl, combine the sour cream, buttermilk, parsley, garlic, black pepper, and salt. Cover and refrigerate until ready to serve.

3   Arrange the corn tortillas on a baking sheet, overlapping them as necessary, and bake uncovered for 8 to 10 minutes. Remove the baking sheet from the oven, stack the tortillas, and loosely wrap them in aluminum foil to keep them warm.

4   Liberally coat a grill pan or large skillet with oil spray, and preheat it over medium heat.

5   Pat the tilapia fillets dry with paper towels. Sprinkle both sides of the fillets with the ancho chile powder and salt.

6   Place the fish on the grill pan or skillet and cook for 2 minutes on the first side. (Work in batches if you can't fit all 4 fillets on the pan at once.)

7   Mist the tops of the fillets with oil spray, flip them over, and cook on the second side for 2 minutes, or until the fish is opaque (it is fine if the fish crumbles at the edges when flipped over). Transfer the fish to a clean platter.

8   To assemble the tacos, use your hands to break the tilapia into big pieces. Divide the fish, greens, and tomatoes among the corn tortillas. Serve the Buttermilk-Parsley Dressing on the side or drizzled on top (about 1 tablespoon per taco). Squeeze the lemon over the fish.

Nutrition Information	Calories – 340 • Protein – 38g • Carbohydrate – 35g • Total fat – 5g
	Saturated fat – 1g • Cholesterol – 85mg • Fiber – 4g • Sodium – 455mg

CREOLE CATFISH
WITH CUCUMBER-RADISH SLAW

Catfish makes a terrific main course. It's low in fat and calories, easy to find, eco-friendly, and reasonably priced. The preparation for this dish couldn't be simpler. Just sprinkle the fillets with zesty Creole seasoning and pan sear to perfection. The refreshing Cucumber-Radish Slaw is the perfect complement to this catfish-with-a-kick. I use a long, slender, seedless English cucumber, which requires no peeling, and mix it with radishes, which I love for their nice peppery bite. The dressing, a simple mix of lemon juice, zest, and salt and pepper, brightens this side dish beautifully. For less than 200 calories per serving, this light yet satisfying meal leaves ample room for dessert!

SERVES 4 (SERVING SIZE: 1 CATFISH FILLET WITH ½ CUP SLAW)

CUCUMBER-RADISH SLAW

1 large English cucumber (unpeeled), coarsely grated

½ teaspoon kosher salt, plus more to taste

1 small bunch (about 6 ounces) radishes, top and bottoms trimmed, cut into matchsticks

Grated zest of 1 lemon (about 1 heaping teaspoon)

Juice of ½ lemon

½ teaspoon black pepper

CATFISH

4 (6-ounce) catfish fillets

1½ tablespoons Creole or Cajun seasoning blend

1 Prepare the slaw: Place the grated cucumber in a strainer set over a bowl or sink. Sprinkle the salt over the cucumber, toss to distribute it evenly, and let stand at room temperature for at least 20 minutes to drain.

2 Place the radishes, lemon zest and juice, and black pepper in a medium bowl; set aside.

3   Pat the catfish fillets dry with paper towels. Generously sprinkle the Creole/ Cajun seasoning on one side of the fillets (you may have leftover spice mixture). Coat the seasoned side of the fillets with oil spray.

4   Liberally coat a large skillet or sauté pan with oil spray, and preheat it over medium heat.

5   Place the catfish fillets in the skillet, seasoned side down, and cook for 2 minutes (any longer and the seasoning mixture is apt to burn).

6   Mist the tops of the fillets with oil spray, flip them over, and cook on the second side for 7 to 9 minutes (depending on the thickness of the fillets), until firm and opaque in the center. (To test for doneness, insert a thin-bladed knife into the center of a fillet to force the flakes apart and verify that the inside is white and opaque.)

7   Meanwhile, finish the slaw: Add the drained cucumber to the bowl of radishes and stir to combine. Season the slaw with additional salt to taste.

8   Serve the catfish fillets with the cucumber slaw on the side.

| Nutrition Information | Calories – 189 • Protein – 31 g • Carbohydrate – 6 g • Total fat – 4 g |
| | Saturated fat – 0.5 g • Cholesterol – 75 mg • Fiber – 1 g • Sodium – 800 mg |

COD AND LENTILS
WITH SMOKED PAPRIKA SOFRITO

Cod is a mild white fish that appeals to even fish-phobic kids. When paired with lentils, the king of legumes (rich in protein, fiber, iron, folate, potassium, and magnesium), you can be sure your family is getting a highly nutritious meal. The base of the dish, sofrito, is a flavorful sauce found mainly in Spanish and Latin cuisines. While it can be made with any number of ingredients, the key seasoning in this version is smoked paprika, an intense spice that really makes the sauce sing. Just before serving, I squeeze fresh lemon juice over the cod to perk up the flavors and tie everything together. Don't leave it out; it really makes a difference.

SERVES 4 (SERVING SIZE: 1 COD FILLET WITH 1 CUP LENTILS AND SOFRITO)

LENTILS

½ cup lentils, rinsed

¼ teaspoon kosher salt

1 bay leaf

COD

1 tablespoon olive oil

1 small onion, finely chopped

2 cloves garlic, minced

1 tablespoon smoked paprika

2 yellow bell peppers, seeded and cut into 1-inch pieces

1 (15-ounce) can no-salt-added diced tomatoes

½ teaspoon kosher salt

4 (6-ounce) cod fillets

½ cup chopped fresh parsley

Juice of 1 lemon

1   In a medium saucepan, combine the lentils, salt, and bay leaf with 1½ cups water. Cover with a tight-fitting lid and bring to a boil. Reduce the heat to low and simmer for 20 minutes or until the lentils are tender.

2   While the lentils are cooking, heat the olive oil in a large skillet over medium heat.

3   Add the onion, garlic, and smoked paprika to the skillet, and cook until the onion becomes translucent, 3 to 4 minutes.

4   Add the yellow bell peppers and cook until they begin to soften, about 5 minutes.

5   Add the tomatoes and ¼ teaspoon of the salt. Bring the sofrito to a simmer and cook until the liquid is reduced by about half.

6   Add the cod fillets and parsley, and sprinkle the remaining ¼ teaspoon salt over the fillets. Reduce the heat to low; the sofrito should be gently simmering. Cover the skillet and cook for up to 15 minutes, or until the cod is cooked through and flaky, adding a tablespoon of water at a time if the sofrito begins to dry out.

7   Drain the lentils, discard the bay leaf, and spoon the lentils around the cod in the skillet. Sprinkle the lemon juice over the cod fillets, and serve.

Nutrition Information	Calories – 327 • Protein – 39 g • Carbohydrate – 32 g • Total fat – 5 g
	Saturated fat – 1 g • Cholesterol – 70 mg • Fiber – 11 g • Sodium – 505 mg

LEMON-DILL SALMON CAKES

If you're looking to get a dose of omega-3s without paying a premium, you've hit the jackpot with this recipe. These salmon cakes use canned salmon rather than expensive fresh fillets. Canned salmon comes with or without skin and bones; I typically buy "with" because it's often cheaper and the extra parts are easy to remove. Be sure to choose cans labeled "wild" or "Alaskan" to minimize contaminants. To further boost the nutritional profile of these delicious patties, I bind them with heart-healthy whole grain oats rather than refined bread crumbs. I love to serve them with a creamy, low-cal sauce made of sour cream, lemon, and fresh dill, all flavors that pair perfectly with salmon.

SERVES 4 (SERVING SIZE: 1 SALMON CAKE WITH SAUCE)

1 (14.75-ounce) can wild salmon, drained, skin and bones removed

½ cup old-fashioned or quick-cooking oats

2 tablespoons skim milk

1 small shallot, finely minced

2 egg whites, beaten

3 tablespoons chopped fresh dill

Grated zest and juice of 1 lemon

½ cup nonfat or low-fat sour cream

Kosher salt and black pepper

1   In a medium bowl, thoroughly mix the salmon, oats, milk, shallot, egg whites, 2 tablespoons of the chopped dill, the lemon zest, and half of the lemon juice. The mixture will be on the wet side, but it will bind up when cooked.

2   Gently shape the salmon mixture into 4 cakes. Transfer the cakes to a plate, and refrigerate for 30 minutes to 2 hours to firm up.

3   While the salmon cakes are resting, prepare the sauce: In a small bowl, combine the sour cream, the remaining 1 tablespoon chopped dill, and the remaining lemon juice. Season with salt and black pepper to taste. Store in the refrigerator until ready to serve.

4   Liberally coat a large skillet or sauté pan with oil spray, and preheat it over medium heat.

5   Place the salmon cakes in the skillet and cook on the first side until golden brown, about 6 minutes.

6   Mist the tops of the cakes with oil spray and then gently flip them over, taking extra care not to break them. Cook for about 4 minutes on the second side, or until the cakes are firm to the touch.

7   To serve, top each salmon cake with a large dollop (about 2 tablespoons) of the sauce.

Nutrition Information	Calories – 205 • Protein – 19g • Carbohydrate – 13g • Total fat – 10g
	Saturated fat – 3g • Cholesterol – 25mg • Fiber – 2g • Sodium – 445mg

BAKED TILAPIA
WITH SPICY TOMATO-PINEAPPLE RELISH

Tilapia is a mainstay in the Bauer house; my kids appreciate its mild taste and flaky texture, while I love its low cost and versatility. Here I top it with a simple pineapple relish that has just three ingredients—and the entire dish is ready to serve in about 20 minutes. The perfectly spiced relish is also tasty on chicken breasts, so if you have more pineapple than you need, refrigerate it and pair the same sauce with chicken later in the week. I like to round out this simple supper with steamed green beans and baked white or sweet potatoes. Fast, fresh, and fabulous!

SERVES 4 (SERVING SIZE: 1 TILAPIA FILLET WITH TOPPING)

4 (6-ounce) tilapia fillets	½ cup well-drained crushed pineapple	1 teaspoon hot chili paste, such as sriracha (or more to taste)
¼ teaspoon kosher salt	1 plum tomato, diced	

1   Preheat the oven to 375°F. Line a baking sheet with aluminum foil, and coat the foil with oil spray.

2   Place the tilapia fillets on the prepared baking sheet and season them with the salt.

3   In a small bowl, combine the pineapple, tomato, and chili paste. Divide the topping evenly among the tilapia fillets.

4   Bake for 12 to 15 minutes, or until the tilapia flakes easily with a fork.

Nutrition Information	Calories – 180 • Protein – 35 g • Carbohydrate – 4 g • Total fat – 3 g
	Saturated fat – 1 g • Cholesterol – 85 mg • Fiber – 0.5 g • Sodium – 235 mg

VEGGIE SIDES

BACON-WRAPPED BRUSSELS SPROUTS

These are the cutest sprouts on the block! I've served them to super-finicky eaters—"Ew! Brussels sprouts? No way!"—and even *they* wind up popping more than a few in their mouths. This can be a side dish or an appetizer, and it's incredibly easy to make (only three ingredients—you can't beat that). Make a batch any time you want your family to get a healthful dose of Brussels sprouts, which boast cancer-fighting properties and provide plenty of soluble fiber to stabilize blood sugar and mood.

SERVES 6 (SERVING SIZE: 4 TO 5 PIECES)

| 1 (9-ounce) container fresh Brussels sprouts | ⅛ teaspoon black pepper | 12 to 14 slices turkey bacon, cut in half |

1   Preheat the oven to 400°F. Line a baking sheet with aluminum foil, and coat the foil with oil spray.

2   Trim the root end of the Brussels sprouts and cut them in half lengthwise.

3   Transfer the Brussels sprouts to the prepared baking sheet, and sprinkle them evenly with the black pepper.

4   One at a time, pick up each sprout and wrap it in a piece of turkey bacon (tuck the edges of the bacon underneath the cut side of the sprout so it will stay put). Place the sprout, cut side down, on the baking sheet. Repeat until all the sprouts have been wrapped in bacon.

5   Bake for 22 to 25 minutes, or until the bacon is crispy.

| Nutrition Information | Calories – 92 • Protein – 6 g • Carbohydrate – 3 g • Total fat – 7 g Saturated fat – 2 g • Cholesterol – 20 mg • Fiber – 1 g • Sodium – 310 mg |

CINNAMON–SUGAR SWEET POTATO FRIES

Crunchy on the outside and soft and creamy on the inside, these delicious oven fries put a smile on the face of everyone who tries them! Nutritionally, sweet potatoes can't be beat, with good amounts of beta-carotene, potassium, and soluble fiber. I dust them with brown sugar and cinnamon to heighten their flavor. (Don't be afraid of the sugar—it's such a small amount and really adds to the final taste and texture of the dish.) Try this recipe and I think you'll see why I often refer to sweet potatoes as "the nutritionist's candy."

SERVES 4

2 medium sweet potatoes (about 1 pound), peeled

¼ cup whole wheat or oat flour

2 tablespoons ground flaxseed

2 tablespoons packed brown sugar

1 teaspoon ground cinnamon

⅛ teaspoon kosher salt

2 egg whites

1   Preheat the oven to 425°F. Liberally coat a large baking sheet with oil spray. (The fries will be crispiest if baked directly on the baking sheet, without aluminum foil.)

2   Cut the sweet potatoes lengthwise into ½-inch-thick slices; then cut each slice into ½-inch-wide strips to form fries.

3   Combine the flour, flaxseed, brown sugar, cinnamon, and salt in a 1-gallon resealable plastic bag. Crumble the ingredients together with your fingertips until they are evenly dispersed.

4   Place the egg whites in a shallow dish and whisk until frothy.

5   Dip the fries into the egg whites; then tap them on the edge of the dish to drain away any excess egg white.

6   Add all the fries to the plastic bag, seal, and shake vigorously to coat the fries evenly with the breading mixture.

7   Delicately remove the fries from the bag and arrange them in a single layer, evenly spaced apart, on the prepared baking sheet. Mist the fries with oil spray.

8   Bake for 15 minutes. Then turn the fries over and bake for an additional 10 to 15 minutes, or until crispy and browned. Let the fries cool slightly before serving to allow the coating to harden.

Nutrition Information	Calories – 148 • Protein – 5g • Carbohydrate – 30g • Total fat – 2g
	Saturated fat – 0g • Cholesterol – 0mg • Fiber – 4g • Sodium – 135mg

CRISPY KALE

Believe it or not, I have heard people liken my Crispy Kale to potato chips. These crunchy pieces of kale are pleasingly salty and utterly addictive, so I completely understand the comparison. When it comes to nutrition, however, the kale wins hands down. This dark leafy green is easy to find year-round and supplies a wealth of nutrients, including vitamin C, beta-carotene, vitamin K, iron, potassium, folate, and of course fiber. A word of caution: Don't start munching on them in the kitchen or they'll never make it to the dinner table!

SERVES 4

1 large bunch kale

Kosher salt

1   Preheat the oven to 400°F. Coat two large baking sheets with oil spray. (The kale will be crispiest if baked directly on the baking sheet, without aluminum foil.)

2   Trim the kale and cut it into 2-inch pieces.

3   Divide the kale pieces between the two baking sheets and spread them out into a single even layer.

4   Liberally mist the kale with oil spray, and lightly sprinkle with salt.

5   Bake for 10 minutes, or until the kale is crispy to the touch and the edges are beginning to brown.

Nutrition Information	Calories: 35 • Protein: 2g • Carbohydrate: 7g • Total fat: 0.5g
	Saturated fat: 0g • Cholesterol: 0mg • Fiber: 1g • Sodium: 150mg

SUMMER SQUASH TIAN

Summer squash is so plentiful in the markets in the summertime, you may run out of ways to serve it. Help is here in the form this lovely, subtle tian that tastes gorgeous paired with delicate pan-cooked fish or a simple chicken dish. Tians are the lighter and more summery cousins of the wintery gratin. This one has a delicate, lemony flavor and is easy to put together, yet impressive enough for company.

SERVES 4 (SERVING SIZE: ½ CUP)

1 tablespoon olive oil

Juice of ½ lemon

½ teaspoon grated lemon zest

1 clove garlic, minced

¼ teaspoon kosher salt

3 plum tomatoes, sliced into ¼-inch-thick rounds

2 medium (yellow or green) summer squash, sliced into ¼-inch-thick rounds

1   Preheat the oven to 400°F. Coat the bottom of a 9-inch round baking dish with oil spray.

2   In a small bowl, whisk together the olive oil, lemon juice and zest, garlic, and salt.

3   Arrange the tomato and squash slices in a circle around the outside edge of the baking dish, tightly overlapping the slices and alternating between 2 slices of squash and 1 slice of tomato. Next, make a second ring of vegetable slices inside the outer ring, using the same overlapping arrangement. Continue this pattern until the entire bottom of the baking dish is covered. (You will need to tightly overlap the slices in order to fit all of them in the dish.)

4   Evenly drizzle or brush the vegetables with the olive oil–lemon mixture. Cover the baking dish with aluminum foil, place it in the oven, and bake for 25 minutes.

5   Remove the aluminum foil. Gently tilt and swirl the pan to redistribute the juices and moisten the vegetables.

6   Bake, uncovered, for 30 more minutes, tilting and swirling the pan to remoisten the vegetables approximately every 10 minutes.

7   When done, the squash will be tender, fragrant, and lightly golden in color. Remove the dish from the oven and let cool for 5 minutes before serving.

Nutrition Information	Calories – 75 • Protein – 3 g • Carbohydrate – 10 g • Total fat – 4 g
	Saturated fat – 0.5 g • Cholesterol – 0 mg • Fiber – 3 g • Sodium – 125 mg

ROASTED CUMIN CAULIFLOWER AND CARROTS

When it comes to vegetable side dishes, I'm all about "no fuss," and few cooking methods are easier—or more delicious, for that matter—than roasting vegetables. Just pop them in the oven and get to work on the rest of the meal while the oven's heat brings out the veggies' natural sugars. Here, carrots add sweetness to cauliflower's mildness, and the color contrast is lovely. Once the cumin's spicy, warm scent fills the kitchen, your mouth will begin to water. This Indian-inspired side dish brings everyday vegetables to a whole new level.

SERVES 4 (SERVING SIZE: 1½ CUPS)

1 medium head cauliflower, cut into florets

6 large carrots, peeled and cut into 1-inch pieces

1 tablespoon ground cumin

½ teaspoon kosher salt

1　Preheat the oven to 400°F. Line a baking sheet with aluminum foil, and coat the foil with oil spray.

2　Spread the cauliflower florets and the carrots in a single, even layer on the prepared baking sheet.

3　Mist the vegetables liberally with oil spray, and sprinkle them evenly with the cumin and salt.

4　Roast for 40 minutes, or until tender.

Nutrition Information	Calories – 83 • Protein – 4g • Carbohydrate – 17g • Total fat – 0.5g
	Saturated fat – 0g • Cholesterol – 0mg • Fiber – 7g • Sodium – 350mg

ROASTED SQUASH
WITH PINE NUTS

I like to make this side dish with kabocha squash, but acorn squash is an equally delicious substitute. Sometimes called "Japanese pumpkin," kabocha tastes sort of like a cross between a pumpkin and a sweet potato. Make sure you have a good sharp knife to cut the squash; but if it's still a little tough, microwave the squash halves for a minute or two to soften them.

SERVES 4

1 large kabocha squash or 2 large acorn squash (about 4 pounds total)

½ teaspoon kosher salt

¼ teaspoon black pepper

2 to 4 tablespoons pine nuts (may substitute chopped pecans or slivered almonds)

1   Preheat the oven to 400°F. Line two baking sheets with aluminum foil, and coat the foil with oil spray.

2   Using a sharp knife, slice the top and bottom off the squash and cut it in half lengthwise. Scrape out all the seeds and fibers.

3   Place the squash, hollowed side down, on the cutting board and slice it into ½-inch-thick half-rings.

4   Arrange the half-rings in a single layer on the prepared baking sheets. Mist the tops with oil spray, and season with the salt and pepper.

5   Bake for 25 minutes.

6   Flip the half-rings over and sprinkle with the pine nuts. Bake for 5 to 10 minutes, or until the squash is tender and the pine nuts are lightly browned (check the oven every few minutes to ensure that the pine nuts do not burn).

Nutrition Information	Calories – 139 • Protein – 4 g • Carbohydrate – 28 g • Total fat – 3 g
	Saturated fat – 0 g • Cholesterol – 0 mg • Fiber – 5 g • Sodium – 250 mg

BALSAMIC-GLAZED PEARL ONIONS

These intensely flavored glazed onions are one of my go-to side dishes. They taste absolutely sensational with roast chicken or just about any meat dish.

SERVES 4 (SERVING SIZE: 1 CUP)

1½ pounds frozen pearl onions

1 tablespoon olive oil

¼ cup balsamic vinegar

1½ teaspoons granulated sugar

¼ teaspoon kosher salt

1   Rinse the onions in cold water for 2 to 3 minutes, until they are mostly thawed. Drain thoroughly; then gently pat dry.

2   Heat the olive oil in a large skillet or sauté pan over medium-high heat until it shimmers.

3   Add the pearl onions and spread them into a single layer in the skillet. Cook without disturbing the skillet until the onions begin to brown, about 5 minutes.

4   Continue to cook, stirring occasionally, until they are golden brown on all sides, 5 to 7 minutes.

5   While the onions are browning, whisk the vinegar, sugar, and salt together in a small bowl.

6   Reduce the heat to medium and carefully add the vinegar mixture to the skillet. Continue to stir until the liquid has completely evaporated and the onions are coated in a deep shiny glaze, about 5 minutes.

Nutrition Information	Calories – 107 • Protein – 2g • Carbohydrate – 18g • Total fat – 3g
	Saturated fat – 0g • Cholesterol – 0mg • Fiber – 2g • Sodium – 180mg

CREAMED SPINACH

This is my healthy interpretation of classic steak-house creamed spinach. I love this side dish for its rich flavor and luxurious texture—and of course because spinach is one of the healthiest foods on the planet. It's loaded with beta-carotene and vitamin C, plus two powerful antioxidants called lutein and zeaxanthin, all of which work together to help maintain sharp eyesight. If you've never cooked fresh spinach before, don't be alarmed by the sheer volume of it. It cooks down quickly, almost magically, right before your eyes. I use shallots for their mellow flavor, which hints of both onion and garlic, and the crushed red pepper adds the perfect amount of zing.

SERVES 4 (SERVING SIZE: ¾ CUP)

1 large shallot, thinly sliced

3 cloves garlic, minced

⅛ to ¼ teaspoon crushed red pepper flakes

2 (10-ounce) bags fresh spinach, large stems removed, leaves roughly chopped

3 ounces (6 tablespoons) low-fat cream cheese

¼ teaspoon kosher salt

1   Liberally coat a large sauté pan with oil spray, and preheat it over medium-low heat.

2   Add the shallot and sauté until tender, about 5 minutes.

3   Add the garlic and red pepper flakes and cook, stirring constantly, for 1 minute.

4   Add as much of the spinach as initially fits. Using tongs or two spoons, start to turn the spinach over in the pan, adding more spinach as it begins to wilt down, until all of the spinach fits in the pan.

5   Continue to cook, stirring constantly, until the spinach has wilted but still has some texture to it, 3 to 5 minutes.

6   Push the spinach off to one side of the pan and add the cream cheese. With the back of a spoon, mash the cream cheese to help it melt. As the cheese melts, pull the spinach into it and continue to stir until the cheese is completely melted and incorporated throughout the spinach.

7   Season with the salt and cook for 3 to 4 more minutes, or until most of the liquids have evaporated. Stir just before serving.

Nutrition Information	Calories – 108 • Protein – 6g • Carbohydrate – 10g • Total fat – 6g
	Saturated fat – 2g • Cholesterol – 10mg • Fiber – 3g • Sodium – 330mg

SLOW-ROASTED TOMATOES

We all know how divine tomatoes taste when they're in season, but there are many months of the year when they are, to put it bluntly, disappointing. I solve the problem by roasting plump little grape tomatoes—which tend to be tastier than others in the off-season—to bring out their sweetness and juiciness. Once you try it, you'll be hooked. It's so easy to perk up the little gems with a short stint in the oven and then either eat them as is, spoon them over grilled fish, or toss them with whole wheat pasta. What's more, cooking the tomatoes releases a potent antioxidant called lycopene, which protects the body against cellular damage. Added bonus: This recipe cooks unattended in under 20 minutes—far less time than it takes me to figure out my daughter's fourth-grade math homework.

SERVES 4 (SERVING SIZE: ½ CUP)

2 (10-ounce) containers grape tomatoes, cut in half lengthwise

1 tablespoon balsamic vinegar

2 teaspoons olive oil

¼ teaspoon kosher salt

⅛ teaspoon freshly ground black pepper

2 large cloves garlic, minced

12 fresh basil leaves, sliced into thin ribbons (optional)

1   Preheat the oven to 450°F. Line a baking sheet with aluminum foil.

2   Place the tomatoes on the prepared baking sheet. Drizzle and sprinkle the remaining ingredients over the tomatoes, and toss thoroughly. Spread the tomatoes out into a single even layer on the baking sheet.

3   Roast for 15 to 20 minutes. Tomatoes can be served hot or at room temperature.

Nutrition Information	Calories – 53 • Protein – 1 g • Carbohydrate – 7 g • Total fat – 3 g
	Saturated fat – 0 g • Cholesterol – 0 mg • Fiber – 2 g • Sodium – 125 mg

SNACKS & SWEETS

CARAMELIZED ONION DIP

Add some healthy pizzazz to your same old crudités platter with this decadent onion dip. My homemade, diet-friendly version is sweetened with slow-cooked caramelized onions and mixed with nonfat sour cream to keep the calories down. It's always a big hit at parties, where I like to serve it with raw vegetables such as carrots, celery, cucumbers, and radishes, or even with small triangles of whole wheat pita bread. Be sure to let the dip mellow for a while in the refrigerator so that the flavors have time to develop.

SERVES 6 (SERVING SIZE: ¼ CUP)

1 tablespoon olive oil

1 large onion, thinly sliced

1 clove garlic, finely minced

½ teaspoon kosher salt

⅔ cup nonfat sour cream

⅓ cup reduced-fat mayonnaise

¼ teaspoon white or black pepper

1 Heat the olive oil in a large skillet or sauté pan over medium heat.

2 Add the onion, garlic, and salt. Cook, stirring occasionally, until the onion is caramelized (golden brown in color), 20 to 25 minutes. Remove from the heat and let cool to room temperature.

3 Transfer the cooled onion mixture to a food processor and pulse until it is finely chopped.

4 Add the sour cream, mayo, and pepper. Pulse until well combined.

5 Cover the dip and refrigerate for at least 1 hour before serving to allow the flavors to blend.

Nutrition Information	Calories – 67 • Protein – 1 g • Carbohydrate – 7 g • Total fat – 4 g
	Saturated fat – 0 g • Cholesterol – 0 mg • Fiber – 0.5 g • Sodium – 315 mg

TANGY GUACAMOLE

These days, guacamole is almost as American as apple pie, although it originated south of the border, where avocados grow abundantly. Avocados are one of those foods blessed with "good fat," a monounsaturated type that boosts heart health and may even help to lower cholesterol. But it's still fat, and all fats—good and bad—are calorific in excess. To counteract this, I cut the avocados with nonfat Greek yogurt, which provides a welcome tang and produces a smooth, creamy dip that meets everyone's expectations. Serve the guacamole with crunchy raw vegetables such as carrots, bell peppers, and sugar snap peas. No one will miss the tortilla chips and your kids will happily eat their veggies (it's a win-win!).

SERVES 8 (SERVING SIZE: ¼ CUP)

2 ripe avocados, peeled, halved, and pitted

½ cup nonfat Greek yogurt (or substitute other nonfat plain yogurt)

½ cup diced cherry tomatoes

½ cup chopped fresh cilantro

½ medium red onion, diced

1 clove garlic, finely minced

1 teaspoon ground coriander

Grated zest of 1 lime

Juice of ½ lime

Kosher salt and black pepper

1   In a medium bowl, mash the avocados and yogurt together to the desired consistency.

2   Stir in the tomatoes, cilantro, onion, garlic, coriander, and lime zest and juice. Season with salt and black pepper to taste.

Nutrition Information	Calories – 90 • Protein – 2 g • Carbohydrate – 6 g • Total fat – 6 g
	Saturated fat – 1 g • Cholesterol – 0 mg • Fiber – 3 g • Sodium – 10 mg

ROASTED RED PEPPER BEAN DIP

Inspired by the intoxicating flavors of Tuscany, this dip is creamy and full-bodied, tasting of sweet roasted red peppers and garlicky, golden olive oil. The beans and peppers make the dip nutrient-dense—red bell peppers are one of the greatest providers of vitamin C in town, while the beans are a terrific vegetarian source of protein and iron. I usually use roasted red peppers packed in brine to minimize calories, but if yours come packed in oil, just be sure to pat them very dry. I think you'll agree this is one of the most glorious dips to ever welcome a stick of raw celery!

SERVES 6 (SERVING SIZE: ¼ CUP)

1 tablespoon olive oil

2 cloves garlic, sliced

2 bottled whole roasted red peppers (5 to 6 ounces), patted dry

1 (15-ounce) can pinto beans, preferably low-sodium, rinsed thoroughly and drained

2 tablespoons grated Parmesan cheese

½ teaspoon crushed dried rosemary

¼ teaspoon kosher salt

Pinch of black pepper

1   Place the olive oil and garlic in a small saucepan or sauté pan. Heat the pan over medium heat for 2 to 3 minutes or until the garlic is lightly golden, taking care not to burn the garlic. Remove from the heat and let cool for 5 minutes.

2   Transfer the cooked garlic and the olive oil to a food processor. Add all the remaining ingredients, and process until smooth.

Nutrition Information	Calories – 95 • Protein – 4 g • Carbohydrate – 13 g • Total fat – 3 g
	Saturated fat – 0.5 g • Cholesterol – 0 mg • Fiber – 4 g • Sodium – 295 mg

BUTTERMILK RANCH DIP

Here's a surefire way to get your family and friends to eat more vegetables. When they dunk raw carrots, sliced zucchini, broccoli florets, or just about any other raw veggie in a low-fat creamy dip, they'll soon be back for seconds, thirds, and fourths! Thin this yummy dip with a little more buttermilk or lemon juice and it doubles as a fantastic ranch salad dressing. The dip gets its richness and tang from the buttermilk, its vibrancy from the scallions and parsley. All around, a winner!

SERVES 8 (SERVING SIZE: ¼ CUP)

1 cup nonfat sour cream

¼ cup reduced-fat mayonnaise

¼ cup nonfat or low-fat buttermilk (shake well before measuring)

Juice of ½ lemon

½ teaspoon kosher salt

¾ teaspoon black pepper

1½ teaspoons onion powder

½ teaspoon garlic powder

2 scallions (white and green parts), thinly sliced

2 tablespoons finely chopped fresh parsley

Combine all the ingredients in a medium mixing bowl, and stir well to combine.

Nutrition Information	Calories – 47 • Protein – 2g • Carbohydrate – 7g • Total fat – 1g
	Saturated fat – 0g • Cholesterol – 5mg • Fiber – 0g • Sodium – 215mg

SLIM-STYLE HUMMUS

Hummus has become a great favorite from coast to coast. In my signature version, I looked for creative ways to lighten up the traditionally high-cal spread made with chickpeas, olive oil, and tahini (sesame paste). Using nonfat Greek yogurt in place of olive oil reduces the calories more than a little without sacrificing the dip's beloved creaminess. Chickpeas, which will always play the starring role in this Mediterranean staple, are a low glycemic food loaded with soluble fiber, which levels out blood sugars and keeps you feeling energized and focused. Feel free to flavor the hummus with anything you fancy while it's whizzing around in the food processor (chopped scallions, roasted garlic, roasted red peppers, or even a sprinkling of crushed red pepper flakes to add some heat). I love to serve this as a dip, but in my house, we just as readily use it in place of mayonnaise on sandwiches or tucked into pita pockets filled with veggies.

SERVES 6 (SERVING SIZE: ¼ CUP)

1 (15-ounce) can chickpeas, preferably low-sodium, thoroughly rinsed and drained

½ cup nonfat Greek yogurt

Juice of 1 lemon

1 clove garlic, minced (or substitute ⅛ teaspoon garlic powder)

1 tablespoon tahini (optional)

¼ teaspoon kosher salt

Black pepper, to taste

Combine all the ingredients in a food processor and process until smooth.

Nutrition Information	*(without tahini)* Calories – 71 • Protein – 5g • Carbohydrate – 13g
	Total fat – 0g • Saturated fat – 0g • Cholesterol – 0mg • Fiber – 4g
	Sodium – 155mg Note: Optional tahini adds 15 calories.

FLAVORED ALMONDS

Almonds are one of my favorite snacks, so I'm always inventing delicious new ways to enjoy them. These super-simple recipes all start with plain natural almonds, which I like to buy in bulk at club stores to save a few dollars. Almonds are a good source of heart-healthy unsaturated fat, and plenty of research suggests they can help to improve cholesterol levels. The cocoa-coated almonds remind me of gourmet chocolate-covered nuts (you know, the kind you once bought for $15 a pound), while the cinnamon-coated ones are completely enrobed in a sugary-sweet glaze. Change directions and ignite your taste buds with the fiery chipotle almonds—just make sure you have a glass of water at your side! I regularly serve all three at parties, and they're always a big hit.

CINNAMON-SUGAR ALMONDS

SERVES 8 (SERVING SIZE: ¼ CUP)

1 egg white

2 cups unsalted raw almonds, skins on

¼ cup packed light brown sugar

1 tablespoon ground cinnamon

⅛ teaspoon kosher salt

1   Preheat the oven to 275°F. Line a large baking sheet with aluminum foil, and coat the foil with oil spray.

2   Whip the egg white in a large bowl until very frothy.

3   Add the almonds to the bowl and stir until they are completely soaked in egg white, about 2 minutes.

4   In a small bowl, stir together the brown sugar, cinnamon, and salt until thoroughly mixed.

5   Add the cinnamon-sugar mixture to the almonds, and stir until the dry ingredients are completely incorporated and evenly coat the almonds (no dry powder should remain at the bottom of the bowl).

6   Pour the almonds onto the prepared baking sheet, and use a spatula, spoon, or your hands to spread them out in a single even layer.

7   Bake for 25 minutes on the middle oven rack.

8   Using a spatula, flip the almonds over in small batches (it's not necessary to flip over every last nut; just make sure you turn the majority of them). Spread the almonds into a single layer and bake for 15 minutes.

9   Remove from the oven and allow to cool for at least 15 minutes. Break the almonds apart with your hands before serving. Store the cooled almonds in an airtight container.

Nutrition Information	Calories – 208 • Protein – 6g • Carbohydrate – 13g • Total fat – 14g
	Saturated fat – 1g • Cholesterol – 0mg • Fiber – 3g • Sodium – 40mg

DARK COCOA ALMONDS

SERVES 8 (SERVING SIZE: ¼ CUP)

1 egg white

1 teaspoon vanilla extract

2 cups unsalted raw almonds, skins on

¼ cup granulated sugar

3 tablespoons unsweetened cocoa powder

⅛ teaspoon kosher salt

1   Preheat the oven to 275°F. Line a large baking sheet with aluminum foil, and coat the foil with oil spray.

2   In a large bowl, combine the egg white and vanilla and whip until very frothy. Add the almonds to the bowl and stir until they are completely soaked in egg white, about 2 minutes.

3   In a small bowl, stir together the sugar, cocoa powder, and salt until thoroughly mixed. Add the sugar-cocoa mixture to the almonds, and stir until the dry ingredients are completely incorporated and evenly coat the almonds (no dry powder should remain at the bottom of the bowl).

4   Pour the almonds onto the prepared baking sheet, and use a spatula, spoon, or your hands to spread them in a single even layer. Bake for 25 minutes on the middle oven rack.

5   Using a spatula, flip the almonds over in small batches and bake for 15 minutes.

6   Cool for at least 15 minutes. Break the almonds apart before serving. Store in an airtight container.

Nutrition Information	Calories – 212 • Protein – 7g • Carbohydrate – 13g • Total fat – 14g
	Saturated fat – 1g • Cholesterol – 0mg • Fiber – 4g • Sodium – 35mg

CHIPOTLE ALMONDS

SERVES 8 (SERVING SIZE: ¼ CUP)

1 egg white

2 cups unsalted raw almonds, skins on

2 tablespoons ground chipotle chile powder

1 teaspoon granulated sugar

½ teaspoon kosher salt

1   Preheat the oven to 275°F. Line a large baking sheet with aluminum foil, and coat the foil with oil spray.

2   Whip the egg white in a large bowl until very frothy. Add the almonds to the bowl and stir until they are completely soaked in egg white, about 2 minutes.

3   In a small bowl, stir together the chipotle powder, sugar, and salt until thoroughly mixed. Add the chipotle mixture to the almonds, and stir until the dry ingredients are completely incorporated and evenly coat the almonds (no dry powder should remain at the bottom of the bowl).

4   Pour the almonds onto the prepared baking sheet, and use a spatula, spoon, or your hands to spread them out in a single even layer. Bake for 25 minutes on the middle oven rack.

5   Using a spatula, flip the almonds over in small batches. Bake for 15 minutes.

6   Cool for at least 15 minutes. Break the almonds apart before serving. Store in an airtight container.

Nutrition Information	Calories – 186 • Protein – 7g • Carbohydrate – 7g • Total fat – 14g
	Saturated fat – 1g • Cholesterol – 0mg • Fiber – 3g • Sodium – 125mg

SOFT-BAKED CHOCOLATE-CHERRY OATMEAL COOKIES

No one argues with cookies, especially not me! These soft, chewy morsels are not only scrumptious but also pretty darn healthful considering they are cookies. I incorporate whole wheat flour and rolled oats to up the fiber and provide an array of vitamins and minerals. Applesauce replaces most of the fat, and adds moisture and good flavor. The semisweet chocolate chips are an indulgence, but the flavanols in the dark chocolate erase most of the guilt. Finally, the antioxidant-rich dried cherries offer natural sweetness and incredible flavor. And as mind-blowing as these are as a snack, they are equally good for breakfast coupled with an egg, yogurt, or a glass of skim milk. How many cookies can make that claim?

SERVES 14 (SERVING SIZE: 2 COOKIES)

1½ cups quick-cooking or old-fashioned rolled oats

½ cup whole wheat flour

½ cup all-purpose flour

½ cup granulated sugar

1 teaspoon baking powder

½ teaspoon baking soda

½ teaspoon kosher salt

⅓ cup semisweet chocolate chips

½ cup dried cherries or dried cranberries

½ cup unsweetened applesauce

1 tablespoon canola oil

2 egg whites, lightly beaten

1 tablespoon vanilla extract

1   Preheat the oven to 350°F. Coat one or two baking sheets with oil spray.

2   In a medium bowl, whisk together the rolled oats, flours, granulated sugar, baking powder, baking soda, and salt until the ingredients are evenly distributed. Add the chocolate chips and dried cherries, and stir to combine.

3   In a large bowl, combine the applesauce, canola oil, egg whites, and vanilla, stirring until smooth.

4   Add the dry ingredients to the applesauce mixture. Stir until just combined and no streaks of flour remain.

5   Drop scant tablespoons of cookie dough onto the baking sheets, and press them lightly with your fingers to flatten the cookies slightly. (To prevent the dough from sticking to your fingers, dip your fingers in water before pressing on the cookies.)

6   Bake for 12 to 16 minutes, or until the cookies start to turn golden brown at the edges. Let them cool on the baking sheets for 3 minutes; then transfer them to a wire rack to cool completely. Store in an airtight container.

Nutrition Information	Calories – 149 • Protein – 3 g • Carbohydrate – 28 g • Total fat – 3 g
	Saturated fat – 1 g • Cholesterol – 0 mg • Fiber – 2 g • Sodium – 135 mg

SILKY PUMPKIN PIE CUSTARDS

I highly recommend this for Thanksgiving—and the other 364 days of the year as well! The custard tastes exactly like pumpkin pie without the crust, and there's zero sense of deprivation. The presentation is just adorable, as they're baked in little individual dishes called ramekins. These single-serving custards cook in a water bath, which is no more complicated to prepare than pouring some hot water into a roasting pan so that it surrounds the ramekins. I like to eat these chilled, but they are also terrific slightly warm from the oven. I must say, finding a decadent dessert with a significant health payoff is like winning the nutritional lottery. And with only 170 calories, plus 2 grams of filling fiber and a hearty dose of beta-carotene to boost your immune system, this luscious pumpkin custard is clearly a winning ticket!

SERVES 6

1 (15-ounce) can 100% pure pumpkin puree

1 cup nonfat milk

½ cup low-fat sour cream

2 large eggs, well beaten

½ cup packed light brown sugar

1 teaspoon ground cinnamon

¼ teaspoon ground ginger

¼ teaspoon ground nutmeg

Pinch of ground cloves

Pinch of kosher salt

1   Preheat the oven to 350°F. Coat six (6-ounce) ovenproof ramekins, custard cups, coffee mugs, or teacups with oil spray.

2   Bring a kettle or pot of water to a boil for use in a water bath.

3   In a large mixing bowl, thoroughly whisk the pumpkin, milk, and sour cream together.

4   Add the beaten eggs to the pumpkin mixture and whisk to incorporate them thoroughly. Then add the brown sugar and all the spices, continuing to whisk well.

5   Divide the pumpkin mixture evenly among the ramekins, making sure to leave at least ¼ inch of space at the top. Place the ramekins in a roasting pan or a deep 13×9-inch baking dish, making sure that the ramekins do not touch each other or the sides of the pan. Transfer the pan to the middle oven rack.

6   Prepare the water bath: Carefully pour boiling water into the roasting pan until the water level reaches halfway up the sides of the ramekins.

7   Bake the custards for 50 to 60 minutes, or until a knife tip inserted into the center of a custard comes out clean.

8   Remove the roasting pan from the oven and allow the custards to cool in the water bath for 20 minutes. Remove the custards from the water bath and serve immediately. If you prefer to serve the custards cold, remove them from the water bath and refrigerate for at least 2 hours before serving.

Nutrition Information	Calories – 170 • Protein – 6g • Carbohydrate – 28g • Total fat – 5g
	Saturated fat – 2g • Cholesterol – 75mg • Fiber – 2g • Sodium – 125mg

BANANA PECAN BREAD

I can't think of a single person who doesn't love banana bread. In my version, I introduce toasted pecans and orange to add another level of tantalizing flavor. Toasting deepens the flavor of the nuts, leaving them extra-scrumptious, so don't forgo that step. Creamy mashed banana supplies plenty of moisture, so there's no need to add a lot of extra fat. To plan ahead, I peel and wrap overripe bananas and stockpile them in my freezer so I can bake this bread at a moment's notice. Gotta love a dessert with just 100 calories per delicious slice, and as an added bonus, ample potassium to keep your blood pressure in check.

SERVES 20 (SERVING SIZE: 1 SLICE)

½ cup pecans

1 cup whole wheat flour

1 cup all-purpose flour

2 teaspoons baking powder

1 teaspoon ground cinnamon

¼ teaspoon ground nutmeg

1½ cups mashed ripe banana (2 large or 3 to 4 small bananas)

2 tablespoons reduced-fat trans-fat-free soft tub margarine spread, at room temperature

½ cup packed light brown sugar

2 large egg whites

1 teaspoon grated orange zest

Juice of 1 small orange

1   Preheat the oven to 350°F. Coat a 9×5-inch loaf pan with oil spray, and set it aside.

2   Spread the pecans in a single layer on a baking sheet. Roast the pecans in the oven until they are lightly toasted, 6 to 8 minutes. Allow them to cool slightly. Then finely chop and set aside.

3   In a medium bowl, whisk together the flours, baking powder, cinnamon, and nutmeg.

4   In a large bowl, thoroughly combine the mashed bananas, margarine spread, brown sugar, egg whites, and orange zest and juice.

5   Sprinkle the dry ingredients over the wet mixture and fold together until the ingredients are just combined. Take care not to overmix; the batter will be slightly lumpy. Gently fold in the pecans.

6   Pour the batter into the prepared loaf pan. Tap the pan on the counter to settle the batter.

7   Bake for 50 to 55 minutes, or until a toothpick inserted into the center of the loaf comes out clean. Cool completely before removing the bread from the loaf pan and transferring it to a plate.

8   Cut the loaf into 10 slices (about ½ inch thick), and then cut each slice in half.

Nutrition Information	Calories – 104 • Protein – 2 g • Carbohydrate – 19 g • Total fat – 3 g
	Saturated fat – 0 g • Cholesterol – 0 mg • Fiber – 2 g • Sodium – 40 mg

BERRY BERRY CRISP

These impressive little desserts are especially delicious when berries are in season, but when they're not, don't hesitate to use frozen berries. In fact, during the off-season months I much prefer frozen to imported "fresh" berries, which cost a small fortune and have been shipped for thousands of miles. The tartness of the apples (I like crisp Granny Smiths for this recipe) complements the sweetness of the berries beautifully. I top the dessert with a mixture of oats, almonds, and wheat bran for crunch and a good measure of fiber. The presentation in individual ramekins is pretty—and provides built-in portion control. While designed as a dessert, the wholesome ingredients make this treat a nutrient-packed breakfast option as well.

SERVES 4

½ cup old-fashioned or quick-cooking rolled oats

2 tablespoons packed brown sugar

2 tablespoons slivered almonds

1 tablespoon wheat bran (or substitute wheat germ or ground flaxseed)

¼ teaspoon ground cinnamon

Pinch of kosher salt

2 tablespoons cold reduced-fat trans-fat-free soft tub margarine spread

3 cups berries (blueberries, raspberries, and/or blackberries), fresh or frozen (see Note)

1 small apple, peeled and grated on the large holes of a box grater

2 teaspoons granulated sugar

1 teaspoon cornstarch

¼ teaspoon grated lemon zest

⅛ teaspoon ground nutmeg

1   Preheat the oven to 350°F. Coat four (6-ounce) ovenproof ramekins, custard cups, coffee mugs, or teacups with oil spray. Place the ramekins on a baking sheet lined with parchment paper or aluminum foil.

2   In a medium bowl, combine the oats, brown sugar, almonds, wheat bran, cinnamon, and salt.

3   Add the cold margarine spread to the oat mixture, and work it in with your fingertips until the margarine is well dispersed and the mixture is crumbly.

4   In a separate medium bowl, mix together the berries, apple, sugar, cornstarch, lemon zest, and nutmeg. Divide the berry mixture equally among the four ramekins.

5   Top each ramekin with the oat mixture.

6   Place the baking sheet in the oven and bake for 20 to 24 minutes, or until the juices are bubbly and the topping is nicely browned. Allow to cool slightly before serving.

NOTE: If using frozen berries, measure the berries frozen, then thaw them slightly before combining them with the other ingredients.

Nutrition Information	Calories – 186 • Protein – 4 g • Carbohydrate – 33 g • Total fat – 6 g
	Saturated fat – 1 g • Cholesterol – 0 mg • Fiber – 9 g • Sodium – 140 mg

CINNAMON CHEESECAKE FONDUE

This recipe is pure fun! Unlike chocolate fondue, it requires no cooking and is not served hot, which means you can whip it up in a flash. This rich, creamy, and inviting dessert is a great way to satisfy a craving for New York–style cheesecake without excessive calories, fat, and sugar. A bowl of this fondue makes the perfect ending to an informal party, and it's also a creative, interactive way to get your kids (and finicky spouses) to eat more fruit. Try apples, strawberries, pears, cantaloupe, honeydew, pineapple, peaches . . . the list goes on forever.

SERVES 4 (SERVING SIZE: ¼ CUP FONDUE)

4 ounces (½ cup) low-fat cream cheese, at room temperature

¾ cup nonfat sour cream

2 tablespoons packed brown sugar

1 teaspoon ground cinnamon

¼ teaspoon vanilla extract

Cut fresh fruit (apples, pears, cantaloupe, honeydew, pineapple, peaches, strawberries)

1   Combine all the ingredients except the fruit in a medium bowl, mixing them vigorously with a whisk until completely smooth. For best results, refrigerate for 30 minutes before serving.

2   Serve with the cut fresh fruit for dipping.

Nutrition Information	Calories – 129 • Protein – 5 g • Carbohydrate – 17 g • Total fat – 5 g
	Saturated fat – 3 g • Cholesterol – 15 mg • Fiber – 0 g • Sodium – 165 mg

TROPICAL SANGRIA

There's nothing like a pitcher of fruity sangria to get the party started! While this doesn't require expensive vino, I suggest a nice, light merlot or a similar wine that you would be happy to drink on its own. My sangria is sweetened with pineapple juice, which, in addition to the fresh fruit, gives the drink its tropical flair. I let the sangria stand in the refrigerator for about 4 hours to allow the flavors to come together (overnight chilling works well, too). Then, just before serving, I stir in a generous amount of lemon-lime seltzer, which cuts the calories while amplifying the drink's fruity flavor. I find this a refreshing alternative to other festive cocktails, which can be extraordinarily caloric—a single frozen margarita, for instance, can run you more than 500 calories. Yikes!

SERVES 4 (SERVING SIZE: 1½ CUPS)

1 (750-ml) bottle red wine

¼ cup orange liqueur, such as Triple Sec or Grand Marnier

1 orange (unpeeled), thinly sliced

1 lime (unpeeled), thinly sliced

1 (8-ounce) can pineapple chunks packed in 100% juice, with juice

2 cups naturally flavored lime or lemon-lime seltzer or club soda

Sliced citrus fruit, for garnish

1   Combine the wine, orange liqueur, orange and lime slices, and the entire can of pineapple, including the juice, in a large pitcher. Stir, and store in the refrigerator for at least 4 hours (or overnight).

2   To serve, strain out the soaked fruit if desired. Pour the chilled seltzer into the pitcher, and stir to combine with the wine.

3   Serve over ice, and garnish with fresh sliced fruit.

Nutrition Information	Calories – 215 • Protein – 0g • Carbohydrate – 12g • Total fat – 0g
	Saturated fat – 0g • Cholesterol – 0mg • Fiber – 0g • Sodium – 10mg

FROZEN HOT CHOCOLATE

Serendipity is a stylish ice cream parlor on the Upper East Side of Manhattan that has been in business for decades and is known for its over-the-top Frozen Hot Chocolate. By my own calculation, each overflowing glass of Serendipity's "fro-ho" packs is over 800 calories, 40 grams of fat, and 22 teaspoons of sugar. (Clearly I was slurping up their fro-hos *before* embarking upon a career in nutrition!) I was determined that this cookbook should include a slimmed-down version of this NYC classic . . . and here it is! This sweet, frothy treat will satisfy your chocolate cravings for only 150 calories and with virtually no fat. Don't forget to try the variations, as they're equally indulgent (the peppermint version tastes like mint chocolate chip ice cream).

SERVES 4 (SERVING SIZE: 1 GENEROUS CUP)

½ cup chocolate syrup

1 cup fat-free evaporated milk

½ teaspoon vanilla extract

3 cups ice cubes

Reduced-fat whipped topping or dark chocolate shavings, for garnish (optional)

1 Combine the chocolate syrup, evaporated milk, vanilla, and ice in a blender and blend until completely smooth.

2 Pour into glasses, and garnish with a dollop of whipped topping or a sprinkling of chocolate shavings if desired.

VARIATIONS: *Mexican Hot Chocolate:* Add ¼ teaspoon ground cinnamon.

Peppermint Hot Chocolate: Substitute ¼ teaspoon mint extract or ⅛ teaspoon peppermint extract for the vanilla extract.

Nutrition Information	Calories – 150 • Protein – 5g • Carbohydrate – 32g • Total fat – 0g
	Saturated fat – 0g • Cholesterol – 0mg • Fiber – 0g • Sodium – 85mg

ACKNOWLEDGMENTS

Sincere thanks to my family, friends, and colleagues—your ongoing support, enthusiasm, and insight helped to make this book a smashing, *delicious* success!

Great, big, gigantic thanks to Johannah McLean, my director of research. Your passion for high-quality, healthy food mixed with sheer commitment and recipe savvy whipped this book into tiptop shape.

To Jane Dystel, Miriam Goderich, Lauren Abramo, and the rest of the crew at Dystel and Goderich Literary Management. I'm able to do what I do because of your ongoing support and guidance.

To everyone at HarperCollins for acknowledging the importance of healthy, home-cooked meals (and for believing in my kitchen skills)! Thanks to my friend and editor, Mary Ellen O'Neill, as well as Michael Morrison, Shelby Meizlik, Kim Lewis, Lorie Pagnozzi, Julia Meltzer, Richard Aquan, and Mac Mackie.

One million thanks to my brutally honest taste-testing squad. To my mom and dad (Ellen and Artie Schloss); my other mom and dad (Carol and Vic Bauer); Ian, Jesse, Cole, and Ayden; the Beal family (Debra, Steve, Ben, Noah, Becca, Chloe, and Jenny); the Schloss family (Pam, Dan, Charlie, Cooper, Glenn, Elena, and Trey); and the Bauer family (Mary, Nat, Jason, Mia, Annabelle, and Harley). Also, many thanks to the countless neighbors and friends *of friends of friends* who were recruited to lend their taste buds along the way!

I'm incredibly grateful to a handful of talented chefs who offered up their culinary expertise: Anna Berman, Mian Catalano, Martha Drayton, Karen Ferries, Anne Haerle, Matthew Hayes, Theresa Marquez, Giovanna Miller, Lauren Costello, and Wendy Wong. And to photographer Joseph DeLeo for making my recipes pop off the page. Also, special thanks to Mary Goodbody.

Infinite appreciation to Susan Turkell, my director of services at Joy Bauer Nutrition. And to the outstanding registered dietitians at Joy Bauer Nutrition—Lisa Mandelbaum, Jennifer Medina, Erica Ilton, Elyssa Hurlbut, Nicole Dilorenzo, Amy Horwitz, Danielle Getty, Laura Wuhl, and Ilyse Shapiro.

To Janice Kaplan, for giving me a comfortable home at *Parade* magazine—it's such a pleasure to work with you.

To Elizabeth Mayhew, Amy Brightfield, and the rest of the staff at *Woman's Day* magazine. It's an honor to be part of your impressive publication.

To my friends at the *Today* show who enable me to improve the health of America. Heartfelt thanks to Jim Bell, Steve Capus, Phil Griffin, Elena Nachmanoff, Don Nash, Noah Kotch, Dee Dee Thomas, Marc Victor, Tammy Filler, Jaclyn Levin, Rainy Farrell, Amanda Marshall, Jayme Baron, Melanie Jackson, Emily Goldberg, Liz Neumann, Lindsay Sobel, Yardena Schwartz, and the countless producers and assistants who help me each week.

And, of course, to the fabulous *Today* hosts: Matt Lauer, Meredith Vieira, Ann Curry, Al Roker, Natalie Morales, Hoda Kotb, Kathie Lee Gifford, Jenna Wolfe, Lester Holt, Amy Robach, Dr. Nancy Snyderman, and David Gregory. Also, thank goodness for everyone in the hardworking stage crew, prop department, wardrobe, hair, makeup, and website.

To Lisa Kussell and Jami Kandell at BWR. You ladies rock!

At *Everyday Health,* my sincere thanks to Ben Wolin, Mike Keriakos, Steven Petrow, Dan Wilmer, Roseann Henry, Debbie Strong, Kristin Vaughan, and Karim Faraq for your hard work and incredible support. You've made it possible for me to help millions of people lose weight, gain health, and improve the quality of their lives.

To my agents at William Morris Endeavor: Strand Conover, Bethany Dick, Ken Slotnick, and Scott Wachs.

And finally, to my husband, Ian, and my three children, Jesse, Cole, and Ayden Jane—I can truly say, the favorite part of my day is coming home after work, whipping up a sensational dinner, and sitting down to a healthy family meal where we share the tales from our day.

INDEX

Note: Page references in *italics* refer to photographs.

A

AJ's Mac-N-Cheezy, *82,* 83–84

Almonds
    Chipotle, *196,* 200
    Cinnamon-Sugar, *196,* 197–98
    Dark Cocoa, *196,* 199

Appetizers and snacks
    Bacon-Wrapped Brussels Sprouts, *172,* 173
    Buttermilk Ranch Dip, 194
    Caramelized Onion Dip, *190,* 191
    Chipotle Almonds, *196,* 200
    Cinnamon-Sugar Almonds, *196,* 197–98
    Dark Cocoa Almonds, *196,* 199
    Roasted Red Pepper Bean Dip, *190,* 193
    Slim-Style Hummus, 195
    Tangy Guacamole, *190,* 192

Apples
    Berry Berry Crisp, 209, *210,* 211

Apricot Almond Oats, 37

Artichokes
    Bite-Sized Chicken Meatball Soup, 48–49
    Turkey Tetrazzini, 85–87

Asian Noodle Soup, *42,* 43–44

Avocados
    Tangy Guacamole, *190,* 192

B

Bacon
    -Wrapped Brussels Sprouts, *172,* 173
    Chicken Cordon Bleu, *124,* 125–26